Mel Bay presents

The Renaissance
VIHUELA *&* GUITAR
in Sixteenth - Century Spain

Luis Milán, Luis de Narváez, Alonso Mudarra,
Miguel de Fuenllana, Enríquez de Valderrábano,
Diego Pisador, and Esteban Daza

The Frank Koonce Series

*Music transcribed
and adapted for
modern guitar,
with facsimiles of the
original tablatures.*

D1616512

MEL BAY ®

1 2 3 4 5 6 7 8 9 0

Visit us on the Web at www.melbay.com — E-mail us at email@melbay.com

Table of Contents

List of Illustrations

Preface

A substantial amount of early music for the guitar remains unknown to modern performers and audiences. In recent years, however, many fine musicologists, scholars, and performers of period instruments have provided a wealth of new materials—facsimile reprints, critical editions, translations of early treatises, and other resources—with which we may now begin to rediscover this music. Nevertheless, many may feel intimidated by the prospect of sorting through and learning to use such resources for the first time. For the uninitiated, just knowing where to start can be difficult.

Scholarly editions, which serve different purposes than performance editions, are not often designed with the modern guitarist in mind. For instance, Renaissance vihuela and lute tablatures are usually transcribed with the open first string as G, not E. Most are presented in double-staff notation, a medium that is superior for realizing counterpoint but unconventional as guitar notation. Furthermore, these editions sometimes give idealized, but not realistic, solutions for voicing, note duration, and other matters that need to be considered within the limitations of our instrument. Guitarists who try to play from these editions essentially are faced with the task of transcribing the transcription!

My idea to create this anthology came about through my own needs in teaching guitar repertoire and history classes at Arizona State University. I also wanted to help bridge the gap between scholarly editions and performance editions by providing a hands-on introduction to tablature transcription and to issues concerning historically informed performance on the modern guitar. I hope that my efforts may be of assistance to other teachers, as well as being simply an attractive collection of music for all to enjoy.

The present volume includes representative selections from the seven books for vihuela that were published in Spain between 1536 and 1576. The reader is strongly encouraged to consult the many excellent publications I have cited and to read directly from the tablatures to experience the rewards of discovery firsthand.

Acknowledgements

As a performer on the modern classical guitar, I am neither a musicologist nor a specialist in early instruments, and so I have relied heavily on the research and expertise of others in preparing this edition. In particular, I want to recognize the remarkable scholarship of John Ward and John Griffiths whose writings are the source for much of my information on vihuela history and stylistic performance. Professor Griffiths has also shared many valuable insights through direct communication with me. I am grateful to Ronald Purcell and Douglas Alton Smith for assistance in developing the text; to Laudon Schuett for proofreading and giving editing suggestions; to Egberto Bermúdez, Joël Dugot, and Carlos González for providing photographic images; to Joan Pellisa for obtaining permission to reproduce artwork; and to Paola Dorsey, Arnoldo García, and James and Margaret Stuhan for help with the Spanish texts and translations. I also wish to thank Al Abrams for photographic services and Sylvain Lemay of Les Productions d'OZ for the music engraving and text formatting. Most of all, I acknowledge Leanne Koonce, my wife and partner, who designed the cover art, provided computer support, and lovingly indulged my obsession with this project.

Development of the Vihuela and Guitar

1.1. The Early Vihuela

There are still many unanswered questions concerning the development of the vihuela prior to the emergence of a written musical tradition. According to John Griffiths, the term "vihuela" in the fifteenth century was used to designate all figure-of-eight shaped stringed instruments that could be played in a variety of ways with a bow, plectrum, or the fingers. He notes that two principal obstacles have hindered our understanding the generic nature of this early instrument:

> Firstly, we have all been too bound by modern classification systems to admit that the one instrument could have been simultaneously a "fiddle," a "viol" and a "guitar." Secondly, we have been too ready to divide early vihuelas into categories of *vihuela de mano* and *vihuela de arco*, terms that are relevant to the purpose-built instruments that started to appear in the 1490s or thereabouts, but not pertinent to earlier instruments.[1]

The first specific reference to a *vihuela de mano* (one which is plucked with the fingers) dates only from the early 1490s, at the court of Ferdinand and Isabella.[2] This time frame coincides with the emerging style of playing polyphonic instrumental music in Spain.

1.2. The Vihuela de Mano

Griffiths provides an overview of Renaissance Spain:

> The marriage of the Catholic Monarchs Ferdinand and Isabella in 1469 produced a hitherto unknown political unity and stability. The reconquest of southern Spain was completed with the capture of Granada in 1492, ending almost eight hundred years of Moorish occupation. The infamous Inquisition was established in 1481, and the expulsion of the Jews in 1492 was also undertaken with the aim of uniting Spain under a single faith. To further imperial aspirations, Columbus' exploratory expedition to the Americas…was financed by Ferdinand and Isabella. Under their rule, Spain emerged as a modern European state.

---

1   John Griffiths, "Extremities: the vihuela in development and decline," in ed. Philippe Canguilhem, et. al., *Luths et luthistes en Occident: Actes de colloque 13-15 Mai 1998* (Paris: Cité de la musique, 1999): 52-53. Griffiths proposes revisions to the historical account provided in Ian Woodfield, *The Early History of the Viol* (Cambridge: Cambridge University Press, 1984).

2   Ibid., 53. The instrument is catalogued by D. Juan Fernández de Oviedo, *Goberno y oficios de la casa del señor principe D. Juan, hijo de los muy altos Reyes Católicos D. Fernando y Doña Isabel* [Seville, 1546], and refers to the prince's chamber in the period before his death in 1497.

The ascent to the throne in 1516 of Charles V, the first Spanish Habsburg, consolidated earlier advances. The Spanish economy was boosted by wealth from the American territories, although this wealth was largely dissipated in wars caused by Charles' religious fervour. Internal stability was maintained, however, and the extension of Spanish sovereignty beyond her national frontiers into Italy, the Low Countries and Africa resulted from Charles' role as Holy Roman Emperor. Spain was a politically dynamic and artistically fertile environment... In 1556 Charles abdicated in favour of his son Philip II. During Philip's reign to 1598, Spain remained at the forefront of European politics and art.[3]

Although the lute was the most popular musical instrument throughout most of Western Europe during the sixteenth century, the *vihuela de mano* flourished in Spain and its colonies alongside the lute. Some scholars have tried to explain the lack of Spanish lute music as a possible rejection of the instrument in preference for the vihuela; however, new evidence suggests that the lute was more commonly played in Spain during the period than previously thought.[4] Nonetheless, what remains indisputable is that the vihuela (and later the guitar) prevailed over the lute in Spanish culture:

> In the last twenty years there has been a fundamental shift in our perception of the social position of the vihuela in sixteenth century Spanish society. Formerly seen as principally an instrument of the court, largely based on evidence suggested by the printed musical sources, recent research makes it clear that the vihuela enjoyed a much wider popularity... The pioneering studies of Pujol and Ward revealed a total of only some thirty-five sixteenth century vihuelists. Subsequent archival research has now quadrupled this figure and articles on many of them are included in the recent *Diccionario de la música española e hispanoamericana*. Furthermore, the discovery of printing contracts for some of the vihuela and related keyboard [music] has made it clear that they were published in large editions of 1000-1500 copies, and were obviously aimed at widespread distribution... Not only do we know of professional vihuelists employed at court, but also of noblemen who were amateur players. Vihuelists from other social groups include university educated professionals and their wives, clerics who played the vihuela in their leisure time, and soldiers such as Garcilaso de la Vega, whose swiftness with the sword was often balanced by skills in poetry and music... The popularity of the vihuela was surely extensive.[5]

Despite this popularity, extant sources of music for the instrument are few. The known repertoire is found in only seven books dedicated specifically to the vihuela, in two books of music considered interchangeable with the harp, lute, and vihuela, and in a handful of unpublished manuscripts.[6]

---

3   John Griffiths, "The Vihuela Fantasia: A Comparative Study of Forms and Styles," (Ph.D. diss., Monash University, Australia, 1984), 2-3.

4   See Douglas Alton Smith, *A History of the Lute from Antiquity to the Renaissance* (The Lute Society of America, 2002), 221-223; also Diana Poulton, "The Lute in Christian Spain" *The Lute Society Journal* 19 (London: 1977): 34-49.

5   John Griffiths, "The Two Renaissances of the Vihuela," online article published by *Goldberg Magazine, www.goldbergweb.com/en/magazine/essays/2005/04/31026.php* (accessed 2 January 2007): 4-6. Griffiths has referenced the work of Emilio Pujol (see footnotes 10, 11, and 12) and of John Milton Ward, "The *Vihuela de mano* and its Music, 1536–1576," (Ph.D. diss., New York University, 1953).

6   The vihuela was also embraced in Italy where there was Spanish influence, especially in Naples and Rome where it was known as the *viola da mano*. See Hiroyuki Minamino, "The viola da mano in Renaissance Italy: A synopsis," *Lute Society of America Quarterly* 34/1 (February 1999): 6-9.

Plate 1	Plate 2

Plate 1

Virgin with Child and angel musicians: detail,
Altarpiece, Colegiata de Játiva (Valencia).
A vihuela with sharply angled waists,
played with a plectrum (*de péñola*).
Photograph: Arxiu Mas

Plate 2

Angel playing a five-course vihuela: detail,
Cathedral de la Santa Creu i Santa Eulalia,
Barcelona. A vihuela with gently curved waists,
played with the fingers (*de mano*).
Photograph: Frank Koonce

1.3. Original Sources of Vihuela Music

Printed Books[7]

1536, Valencia. Luis Milán. *Libro de música de vihuela de mano, intitulado El maestro.*[8]

1538, Valladolid. Luis de Narváez. *Los seys libros del delphin, de música de cifras para tañer vihuela.*[9]

1546, Seville. Alonso Mudarra. *Tres libros de música en cifras para vihuela.*[10]

---

7   Locations of copies and lists of their contents are given in Howard Mayer Brown, *Instrumental Music Printed before 1608: A Bibliography* (Cambridge, MA: Harvard University Press, 1967).

8   Facsimile edition: (Geneva: Éditions Minkoff, 1975). Critical editions: ed. Leo Schrade (Leipzig: Publikationen Älterer Musik 2, 1927), reprint ed. Georg Olms (Hildesheim: 1967); ed. Charles Jacobs (University Park and London: Penn. State Univ. Press, 1971); ed. Ruggero Chiesa, in guitar notation and pitch (Milan: Edizioni Suvini Zerboni, 1974).

9   Facsimile edition: (Geneva: Éditions Minkoff, 1980). Critical editions: ed. Emilio Pujol (Barcelona: Instituto Español de Musicología, *Monumentos de la Música Española* 3, 1945, reprint 1971). Although informative, this edition is difficult to use because Pujol's transcriptions are in keys that had only been "imagined" in the original tablatures. He had mistakenly believed that the clefs in the original tablature indicated vihuelas of different sizes, whereas the clefs simply were intended to help the performer locate the *final* of the mode that was transposed from its original pitch [see 5.1]; ed. Rodrigo de Zayas (with facsimile), *Los vihuelistas: Luys de Narváez* (Madrid: Editorial Alpuerto, *Colección Opera Omnia*, 1981); ed. Eduardo Martínez Torner (Madrid: Orfeo Tracio, *Colección de Vihuelistas Españoles del Siglo 16*, 1923, reprint (Madrid: Unión Musical Española, 1965); and, in guitar notation and pitch, ed. Graciano Tarragó (Madrid: Unión Musical Española, 1971).

10 Facsimile edition: (Monaco: Editions Chanterelle, 1980). Critical edition: ed. Emilio Pujol (Barcelona: Instituto Español de Musicología, *Monumentos de la Música Española* 7, 1949, reprint 1984).

1547, Valladolid. Enríquez de Valderrábano. *Libro de música de vihuela, intitulado Silva de nas.*[11]

1552, Salamanca. Diego Pisador. *Libro de música de vihuela.*[12]

1554, Seville. Miguel de Fuenllana. *Libro de música de vihuela, intitulado Orphénica lyra.*[13]

1576, Valladolid. Esteban Daza. *Libro de música en cifras para vihuela intitulado El parnasso.*[14]

Manuscripts

The oldest known vihuela tablature is a single, one-page piece found in a copy of Lucius Marineus Siculus' *Epistolarum familiarum* (Valladolid, 1514), held by the British Library under the shelf mark C.48.h.1.[15]

Madrid, Biblioteca Nacional, MS 6001 is a collection of ten pieces, discovered in 1975 by Juan José Rey in a poetic anthology called *Ramillete de flores* (1593).[16]

The "Simancas Fragments," is a recently discovered collection of seven pieces held at the Archivo General de Simancas, Casa y Sitios Reales, leg. 394, fol. 130-31.[17]

The "Barbarino" lutebook, Cracow, Biblioteka Jagiellonska (olim Berlin) Mus. MS 40032 is a substantial collection believed to have been compiled in Naples ca. 1590 to 1611.[18]

---

11 Facsimile edition: (Geneva: Éditions Minkoff, 1981). Critical edition: ed. Emilio Pujol (Barcelona: Instituto Español de Musicología, *Monumentos de la Música Española* 22-23, 1965).

12 Facsimile edition. (Geneva: Éditions Minkoff, 1973). Critical edition with facsimile: ed. Juan Carlos Duque, transcriptions by Francisco Roa and Felipe Gértrudix (Madrid: Editorial Pygmalión 3 vols., 2002).

13 Facsimile edition: (Geneva: Éditions Minkoff, 1981). Critical edition: ed. Charles Jacobs (Oxford: Oxford University Press, 1978).

14 Facsimile edition: (Geneva: Éditions Minkoff, 1979). Critical editions: *Esteban Daza: The Fantasias for Vihuela*, ed. John Griffiths (Madison: A-R Editions, *Recent Researches in Music of the Renaissance* 54, 1982); and *Los vihuelistas: Esteban Daça*, ed. Rodrigo de Zayas (Madrid: Editorial Alpuerto, *Colección Opera Omnia*, 1983).

15 Reproduced by Antonio Corona-Alcade, "The Earliest Vihuela Tablature: A Recent Discovery," *Early Music* 20 (1992), 594–600. Corona-Alcade provides a facsimile, transcription, and historical analysis.

16 Facsimile editions: Juan José Rey, ed., with critical notes and transcription (Madrid, 1975); and Javier Hinojosa and Frederick Cook, ed. (Zurich: Editio Violae, 1981). This collection contains nine previously unknown works and a variant of *Guárdame las vacas* by Narváez.

17 Reproduced by Antonio Corona-Alcalde, "A Vihuela Manuscript in the Archivo de Simancas," *The Lute* 26 (1986): 3-20. A full-size color facsimile and transcription of this manuscript edited by Antonio Baciero has been published in the series Colección el Mundo de Felipe II (Madrid: Testimonio, 1998).

18 See John Griffiths, "Berlin Mus. MS 40032 y otros nuevos hallazgos en el repertorio para vihuela," in *España en la Música del Occidente*, ed. Emilio Casares et al., 2 vols. (Madrid, 1987), vol. 1, 323-324. This manuscript, previously held by the Preussiche Staatsbibliothek, Berlin, was lost after World War II and was rediscovered at the Jagiellonian Library in Cracow. It is being evaluated by Griffiths and other specialists.

Manuscripts are also found attached to individual copies of three of the printed books: the Madrid copy of Mudarra's *Tres libros*,[19] one of the Madrid copies of Valderrábano's *Silva de sirenas* (R. 14018),[20] and in the Vienna copy of Valderrábano's book.[21]

Other Sources

Two printed sixteenth-century books were designated as being suitable for any polyphonic Instrument:

> 1557, Alcalá de Henares, Spain. Luis Venegas de Henestrosa, *Libro de cifra nueva para tecla, arpa y vihuela.*[22]

> 1578, Madrid. Antonio de Cabezon, *Obras de música para tecla, arpa y vihuela.*[23]

1.4. The Four-Course Guitar

The *guitarra de cuatro órdenes* was a treble instrument, smaller than the vihuela and easier to play. Although initially played with a plectrum, images dating from the sixteenth century usually show players plucking with their right-hand fingers. This indicates the evolution of technique to accommodate polyphonic music and strumming patterns.

Plate 3
Angel playing a four-course guitar.
Polychrome wooden carving,
Museo Catedralicio, Ávila.
Photograph: Carlos González

19   This copy has ten handwritten pages with six pieces copied from Fuenllana's *Orphénica lyra* and a previously unknown piece entitled *basa e alta.*

20   This book has four handwritten pages containing four pieces copied from Fuenllana's *Orphénica lyra.*

21   This manuscript consists of three sets of *diferencias* by an unknown author.

22   Critical edition: *La música en la corte de Carlos V con la transcripción del "Libro de cifra nueva para tecla, harpa y vihuela" (Alcalá de Henares, 1557) compilado por Luys Venegas de Henestrosa*, 2 vols., ed. Higinio Anglés (Barcelona: Instituto Español de Musicología, *Monumentos de la Música Española* 2-3, 1944; reprint 1965).

23   Critical edition: *Antonio de Cabezón: Obras de música para tecla, harpa y vihuela... Recopiladas y puestas en cifra por Hernando de Cabezón su hijo*, ed. Felipe Pedrell, rev. Higinio Anglés (Barcelona: Instituto Español de Musicología, *Monumentos de la Música Española* 27-29, 1966).

More than three hundred pieces are known to have been written for the four-course guitar, the majority appearing outside of Spain in French and Flemish publications. The earliest guitar pieces, however, are from Spain and are found in two of the vihuela books. The first six are from 1546 in Alonso Mudarra's *Tres libros de música en cifras para vihuela*. Eight years later, nine more guitar pieces appeared in Miguel de Fuenllana's *Orphénica lyra*—with nine other works for a five-course instrument that Fuenllana called the *vihuela de cinco ordenes*. This is likely the same instrument that later became known as the *guitarra de cinco ordenes* [see 2.3]. The popularity of the five-course guitar rapidly eclipsed that of the four-course guitar following the publication of a tutor by Joan Carles Amat in 1596. It also popularized the *rasgueado* style of playing chords for the accompaniment of songs and dances.[24]

1.5. Facsimile Edition on CD-ROM

The first complete digital edition in facsimile of all seven of the published Spanish books of vihuela and guitar music is now available on one CD-ROM. Compiled by Carlos González, Gerardo Arriaga, and Javier Somoza, this excellent resource includes over seven hundred works in an easily accessible format. Furthermore, the original red numerals (*cifras coloradas*) of pieces with vocal parts are preserved, whereas other printed facsimiles are in monochrome and thus obscure the vocal line. The reader is encouraged to use this disc to view all facsimile images of the tablatures not shown in the present anthology.[25]

Plate 4
Engraving of the prophet Eliseus (Elisha), from Mudarra's *Tres libros de música*.

---

24 The earliest extant copy of Amat's book is a 1626 version, published in Lérida and entitled *Guitarra española de cinco ordenes la qual enseña de templar, y tañer rasgado todos los puntos…* (The Spanish guitar of five courses, which teaches tuning and all the chords for playing in strummed fashion). The treatise was revised and published again in Saragossa in 1639, and many times thereafter.

25 *Libros de Música para Vihuela, 1536-1576*, CD-Rom001 (Ópera Tres and Música Prima: Spain, 2003).

2

Tunings of the Vihuela and the Guitar

The vihuela usually had six pairs of strings—referred to as courses—although five-course and seven-course variants existed alongside the six-course "common" vihuela (see the cover art of this edition).[26] All the strings were made of gut since wound bass strings did not become available until the middle of the seventeenth century. (The frets also were made of gut and were tied around the neck, which allowed fine tuning adjustments to be made by shifting their position on the fingerboard. This also helped compensate for imperfections of gut strings and for refining intonation according to the mode in which the piece was written.) The upper courses were tuned as unison pairs. The same is probably true for the lower courses although there is no hard and fast evidence that would exclude the practice, common among lutenists, of using octave stringing for added harmonic color and duration.[27]

2.1. Tunings of the Six-Course Vihuela

According to Bermudo in 1555, the vihuela was tuned in fourths, with the exception of one major third between the third and fourth courses.[28] He provides the following fingerboard diagram [Plate 5]:

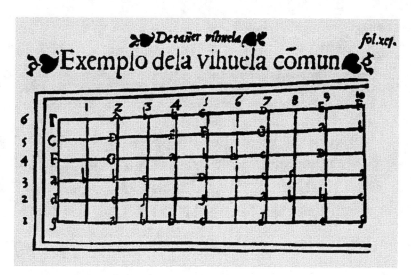

Plate 5
Engraving of the "common" vihuela fingerboard, from Bermudo's *Declaración*.

---

26 The term "course" (Spanish: *órdenes*) is used to refer to a grouping of strings (usually two) tuned in unison or an octave apart, and played together as though they were one string.

27 See William Ahern, "Playing Devil's Advocate: The Shaky Case for Unison-Course Vihuela Stringing." *Lute Society of America Quarterly 29/3* (1994): 3-10; reply by Donald Gill: *LSA Quarterly 30/1* (February 1995): 29-30; and rebuttal by Hearn in *LSA Quarterly 31/2* (May 1996): 16-18. Further communication by Gill in *LSA Quarterly 31/4* (November 1996): 4-5.

28 Juan Bermudo, *El libro llamado declaracion de instrumentos musicales* (Osuna, 1555; facsimile reprint, Kassel: Bärenreiter, 1957), Spanish theorist Juan Bermudo provides much of the information we have today about early instruments and performance practices. The section entitled "De tañer vihuela" (On playing the vihuela) has been translated into English, with a detailed introduction, by Dawn Astrid Espinosa, *Journal of the Lute Society of America* 28-29 (1995-1996), 3.

The lowest tone on the open sixth course is represented in the diagram by the character for the third letter of the Greek alphabet, *Gamma*—the lowest note in ancient Greek and medieval music theory. This pitch, which corresponds to G, is only hypothetical—or "nominal" (in name only)—because pitch at that time was not standardized. Actual pitch was determined by the size of the instrument and tension limits of the gut strings. This pitch was later referred to as *Gamma-ut* or *Gamut*.[29]

To facilitate the transcription of music written in mensural staff notation so that it could be placed comfortably on the fingerboard, Bermudo advises the player to "imagine" the instrument being pitched to fit the mode of the music. Modal theory, unlike our modern tonal system, associated the names of pitches—although nominal—and their intervallic relationships with specific modes. Therefore, the modern concept of transposing music to fit the instrument was not theoretically possible. Instead, the instrument was made to fit the music. Bermudo explains that the player "imagines, then, that the vihuela sometimes begins on *Gamut* [G], other times on *A re* [A]…"[30] Thus, the first mode, Dorian (D–d), would begin on the fifth interval above a vihuela imagined to be pitched in G, and on the fourth interval above a vihuela imagined to be pitched in A [see 5.2].[31]

Vihuela tunings "imagined" to be pitched in G and A

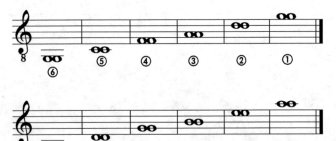

Later in the book, Bermudo provides additional diagrams showing other "imagined" pitches to which vihuelas could be tuned. The lowest pitch of the music determined the pitch of the lowest course.

---

29 The term eventually came to mean the entire scale and, in fact, the complete range of anything.

30 Bermudo (fol. 90ᵛ), 2.

31 See John M. Ward, "Changing the Instrument for the Music," *Journal of the Lute Society of America* 15 (1982): 31.

2.2. Tunings of the Four-Course Guitar

For the four-course guitar, Bermudo gives two tunings: *temple a los nuevos* (new tuning)—with the interval pattern of a fourth, major third, fourth, and the lowest course tuned as *g*; and *temple a los viejos* (old tuning)—with the lowest course a whole step lower, *f*, to make a perfect fifth below the third course.

temple a los nuevos

temple a los viejos

In comparing the guitar to the vihuela, Bermudo writes:

> A player can better display his skill with the understanding and use of the guitar than with that of the vihuela, because it is a smaller instrument.[32]

However, he then notes:

> All four strings [i.e., courses] on the guitar *a los nuevos* are in the [same] tuning and disposition as the four of the common vihuela, that is, with the sixth and the first strings removed. I mean that if you want to make a vihuela into a guitar *a los nuevos*, take off the first and sixth strings. And if you want to make the guitar into a vihuela, put a sixth and a first string on it. Often people place another string on the fourth course of the guitar [so] that…both strings form an octave.[33]

It is significant that Bermudo has chosen to compare the tuning of the two instruments this way instead of simply saying that the third course of the guitar is tuned a half step higher than on the vihuela in A-tuning. By using the top four courses of the vihuela and re-tuning the third course, it would be possible to duplicate not only the interval pattern but also the relative pitch of the smaller guitar. It seems, therefore, that pitch—and by extension, size—did not have much importance to Bermudo as a distinguishing characteristic between the two instruments.

---

32 Bermudo, ch. 65, fol. 96^R, 39. *De mayor abilidad se puede monstrar un tañedor con la intelligencia, y uso de la guitarra: que con el de la vihuela, por ser instrumento más corto.*

33 Ibid., 40. *La guitarra a los nuevos tiene todas cuatro cuerdas en el temple, y disposición de las cuatro de la vihuela commun: que seran, sacadas la sexta y prima. Digo, que si la vihuela quereus hacer guitarra a los nuevos: quítale la prima y sexta, y las cuatro cuerdas que le quedan: son las de la guitarra. Y, si la guitarra quereys hacer vihuela: ponedle una sexta y una prima. Suelen poner a la cuarta de la guitarra otra cuerda, que…forman ambas cuerdas una octava.*

2.3. Development and Tunings of the Five-Course Vihuela

The practice described above may have helped lead to the creation of a variant type of vihuela with five courses. This instrument is known to have existed as early as the middle of the sixteenth century. The earliest surviving publication to include works for the "vihuela de cinco ordenes" was by Miguel de Fuenllana, in his book *Orphénica lyra*, of 1554. Fuenllana's tablature indicates an instrument having a third course that is a half step higher than on the six-course vihuela.

Pictorial records of five-course vihuelas show an instrument more or less identical in size to the standard vihuela. Together with Bermudo's comments on tuning, one can surmise that the five-course vihuela's pitch and tuning were like those of a standard vihuela without the first course.

Five-Course Vihuela Tuning, Pitched in A

As previously mentioned, the general belief held today is that unison tuning was standard practice on the six-course vihuela, but we do not know this for certain. Since octave tuning was used for the fourth course of the guitar, and later for the five-course guitar, it seems plausible that octaves came to be used for the five-course vihuela eventually, if not from the beginning:

Tuning of the Five-Course Vihuela with Octave Basses

2.4. Transition to the Five-Course Guitar

A widely held assumption today is that the so-called "Baroque" five-course guitar was the result of adding a fifth course to the four-course "Renaissance" guitar. However, when one takes into account the practices described by Bermudo and the gradual hybridization of the vihuela and guitar, the five-course vihuela would seem to have all of the essential characteristics in place—size, pitch, and tuning—to suggest that this instrument was the progenitor of the five-course guitar.

– 3 –
Surviving Instruments

3.1. The "Guadalupe" Vihuela. Until recently there was only one known surviving vihuela, which is now in the Jacquemart-André Museum in Paris. This is an unusually large instrument, possibly a luthiers' guild examination masterpiece, and therefore not representative of the common vihuela design. It is constructed of many small parts of contrasting dark and light wood that are glued together in intricate designs. The word "Guadalupe," which is burnt into the peg box with a branding iron, may indicate that the instrument was made by Joan de Guadalupe, a *violero* ("maker of viols") in Toledo ca. 1525. An inscription in the soundboard indicates that it was used in a later period as a five-course guitar.

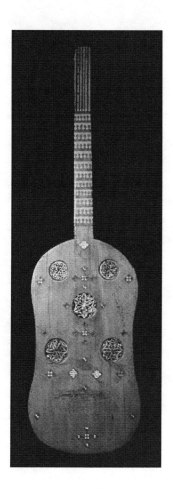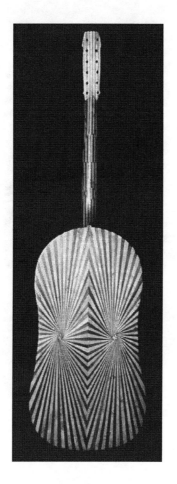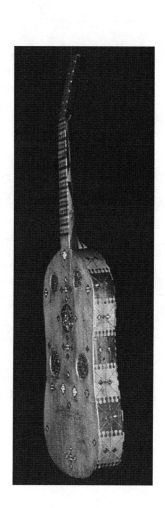

Plate 6
The "Guadalupe" Vihuela
Jacquemart-André Museum, Paris
Photograph: Carlos González

3.2. The "Quito" Vihuela. An instrument that some believe to be a vihuela was discovered in 1976 at the Iglesia de la compañía de Jesús in Quito, Ecuador. Examination of it has been difficult because it is protected as a holy relic of Santa Mariana de Jesús (1618-1645).[34] Now often referred to as the "Quito" vihuela, evidence suggests that it had been made locally ca. 1625 using European design principles from the previous century.

Plate 7
The "Quito" Vihuela (?)
Iglesia de la compañía de Jesús, Quito, Ecuador
Photograph: Egberto Bermúdez

---

34 Egberto Bermúdez, "The Vihuela: The Paris and Quito Instruments," *La Guitarra Española*, (Madrid: Museo Municipal; and New York: Metropolitan Museum of Art, 1991-2), 24-47.

3.3. The "Chambure" Vihuela. An instrument that is referred to as the "Chambure" or the "Paris" vihuela was re-discovered by museum curator Joël Dugot in 1996 and first drawn to public attention in 1998. Having been given by the late Geneviève Thibault, Comtesse de Chambure, it had lain forgotten in the depot of the old Paris Conservatoire collection. Now in the Musée de la Musique, Paris, this is perhaps one of the most important organological discoveries of the past few decades. This instrument has a vaulted and ribbed back (ribs that are curved in both directions) of similar construction to an instrument in the collection of the Royal College of Music, London [see 3.4].

Plate 8
The "Chambure" Vihuela (?)
Photograph: Publimages, T.R.
Musée de la Musique (Paris)

3.4. The Dias Guitar or Vihuela. A small instrument that is now in the collection of the Royal College of Music, London, has a label inside that translates as "Belchior Dias made me. / Lisbon month of December 1581."[35] Opinions differ as to whether this is a small five-course guitar, a *vihuela de cinco órdenes* as described by Bermudo [see 2.3], or even a six-course vihuela.[36] Other musicologists and organologists argue that these distinctions in design and stringing are irrelevant, and that the terms "guitar" and "vihuela" were interchangeable at this time.

 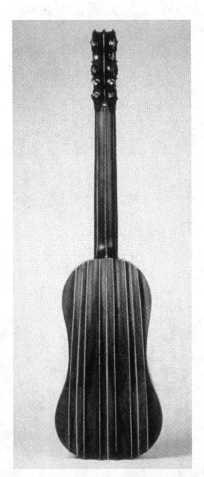

Plate 9
A vihuela or guitar by Belchior Dias
Collection of the Royal College of Music, London
Photograph: Carlos González

35 This instrument closely resembles the only other sixteenth-century guitar known to exist, which is now in the possession of the author. See Frank Koonce, *The Baroque Guitar in Spain and the New World,* (Pacific, MO: Mel Bay, 2006), 6.

36 Because of an extra hole in the headstock, luthier Alexander Batov argues that this instrument is a six-course vihuela in two online articles: "The vihuela and guitar crossroads: looking for evidence," *www.vihuelademano.com/vgcrossroads.htm*; and "The Royal College Dias - guitar or vihuela?," *www.vihuelademano.com/rcmdias.htm* (accessed 6 May 2007). Luthiers Stephen Barber and Sandi Harris argue against this theory and provide reasons why they think it is a small five-course guitar: *www.lutesandguitars.co.uk/html/cat12.htm* (accessed 6 May 2007).

—4—
Reading and Transcribing Tablature

The word "tablature" comes from the Latin noun *tabula* (table), and refers to a form of notation that graphically represents where notes are played on an instrument. Three main types of tablature were used for plucked fretted instruments during the Renaissance, which now are usually referred to as French, Italian, and German. By 1600, however, the more complex German system had largely disappeared while the French and Italian ones persisted.

Anyone today who wishes to perform early music for the guitar and other fretted instruments should learn to read tablature because it provides direct access to the original, unaltered, music. Through tablature, performers also gain access to the vast quantities of Renaissance and Baroque pieces that have not yet been transcribed. Those arguments notwithstanding, there are benefits to having tablature transcribed into modern notation. Transcriptions facilitate the playing of music on instruments other than those for which it was written, and modern notation enables performers to see functional aspects of the music such as pitch relationships, voicing, and harmonic structures. Modern notation also provides an introduction to the performance of early music for those not yet accustomed to reading tablature.

Nevertheless, the conversion of tablature into modern notation involves making many subjective choices on matters such as note duration and voicing; therefore, even the most conscientious transcriber cannot avoid imparting personal preferences into this process. Transcriptions that try to accommodate the tuning of a modern guitar are especially problematic. These often result in something far removed from the original voicings, articulations, and textures suggested by the tablature.

It also must be understood that editors may have perspectives that fall anywhere between two diametric extremes. At one end, an editor may disregard information provided in the tablature and try to improve the music by revising or even re-composing much of it. At the other end, an editor may try to represent an imagined ideal of performance that goes beyond realistic technical capabilities of the instrument.

In summary, one must realize that any editorial solution may represent only one of many interpretative possibilities and may therefore hinder the reader from exploring alternatives that are equally valid—or even more so. Given all of the ambiguities of tablature notation and the subjectivity associated with the transcription process, players should always consult the tablature for the most direct connection to the original music.

4.1. Pitch

Vihuela and four-course guitar music from Spain and Italy is written in Italian tablature. The lines of the tablature "staff" represent the strings or courses of the instrument: six for the standard vihuela, five for the five-course vihuela, and four for the guitar. The bottom line represents the first (highest-pitched) course. In this layout, the tablature projects a mirror image of the strings when the music is placed on a table for reading. In Spain, the only known exception to this practice is the tablature of Luis Milán, which has the highest course represented by the top line.

Numbers placed on the lines indicate the frets that are to be stopped on a particular course to produce the desired notes. The number 0 represents the open course, 1 is for the first fret, 2 for the second fret, and so on. To represent the tenth fret, the Roman numeral X is used, instead of the Arabic 10, to avoid it being misread as two notes.

4.2. Time Values

Mensural notation symbols are placed above the staff to indicate the duration of each note or chord. These symbols indicate the amount of time before another note must be played. They do not necessarily indicate actual sustain of individual notes, which may overlap in different voices. The following table relates the old symbols to their graphically similar modern equivalents:

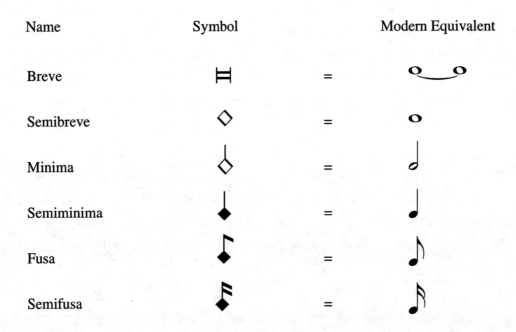

Name	Symbol		Modern Equivalent
Breve		=	
Semibreve		=	
Minima		=	
Semiminima		=	
Fusa		=	
Semifusa		=	

Milán provides a separate symbol over every numerical change in the tablature (as shown below). In all subsequent vihuela publications a symbol is given only when the time value changes.

Pavana No. 2, Luis Milán
(Tablature with the highest-pitched course on the top line):

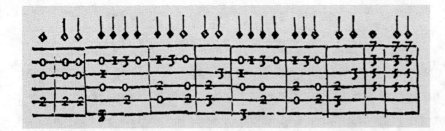

16

4.3. Literal and Interpretative Transcriptions

There have been two basic approaches to transcription. The first is a "literal" (objective) transcription that reflects nothing more than what is actually provided by the tablature. The example below is a literal transcription of the Milán tablature excerpt.

The second is an "interpretive" (subjective) transcription that provides a plausible realization of the music into individual voice lines and that assigns longer note values to the slower-moving voices.

Interpretive transcriptions have generally become the most favored method because they convey the sense of the music: they reflect both the polyphony and functional harmony (such as the suspensions in measures 4-5 and 7-8 of the preceding example) that would be heard in performance.

4.4. Barlines and the Compás

Spanish Renaissance tablatures have barlines that appear to divide notes into measures as in modern staff notation. These groupings are not measures in the modern sense of the word, but simply units that show which are the down and up beats. In the sixteenth century this was known in Spanish as *compás*—or *tactus* in Latin. Milán says this is what results when you "raise and lower the hand or foot for an even tempo."[37] The *compás* functions simply as a method for counting, and is not intended to provide an indication of accents. In other words, the downbeat of a *compás* is not necessarily accented. While the *compás* may correspond satisfactorily to the modern measure in some tablatures, two or more may need to be grouped together in others to represent the best metrical organization of the piece. The choice of a suitable meter is often the most challenging aspect of making a transcription of this music. The factors to consider in this process are discussed below.

---

37 Luis Milán, *El Maestro*, xvii, trans. Ward, "Vihuela de mano," 67.

4.5. Tactus Reduction

Today, we are accustomed to using smaller values than those usually found in vihuela tablature: the semibreve conforms more closely to our modern half note or quarter note instead of the graphically similar whole note. Therefore, most editors use some degree of "tactus reduction" in a modern transcription. For example, a 2:1 reduction means that the semibreve is transcribed as a half note.

The downbeat and upbeat of a single two-part *compás* sometimes may serve as the two beats of a modern metrical measure as shown above. On the other hand, some transcribers may choose to combine two or more *compases* into larger groupings.

4.6. Multimetric and Non-Metric Transcription

Because Renaissance music was not organized according to our modern concept of recurring metrical patterns, it often resists being transcribed neatly into consistent and equal measures that are larger than the original *compás*. In the previous example, for instance, with two *compases* equal to the modern measure, a repeated rhythmic structure in measure 3 occurs on a different beat than when first stated in measure 2, thereby seeming to contradict the established metrical pattern. Theorist Paul Creston tells us that this is nothing more than rhythmic "overlapping"—a phrase rhythm that extends beyond the barline. According to Creston, accent is not an element of meter, which is just the measurement of duration, and that it is a twentieth-century misconception to believe that the first pulse of a measure is always strong. Through the principle of overlapping, the phrase rhythms can cross the metric barlines, the effect being changes of meter without a change in the metric notation.[38]

---

38 Paul Creston, *Rational Metric Notation: The Mathematical Basis of Meters, Symbols, and Note-Values* (Hicksville, NY: Exposition Press, 1979), 13.

Nevertheless, some theorists describe this type of music as being "multimetric," and may choose to write metric changes to better accommodate the rhythmical structures.[39]

Creston acknowledges that metric changes are sometimes warranted, although he strongly discourages their overuse. Furthermore, as pointed out by David Grimes, multimetric notation is often subject to varying interpretations and "can lead to extremely convoluted and tortuous attempts to force [this] free-flowing music into artificial units."[40] Grimes prefers to use an unmeasured notation—a staff without a meter signature and barlines (together with 4:1 tactus reduction).

4.7. Hemiola and Syncopation

One highly characteristic aspect of Spanish music is the "hemiola," a change to two equal beats against a meter of three pulses, or vice-versa—three beats against two pulses. This often gives the effect of syncopation—stressed or accented notes that go against the established metrical pattern. Another way to look at hemiola is as an alternation between duple and triple meter. In other words, it may be considered a momentary metric change rather than a change of the beat pattern against an unchanging meter. For pieces that frequently alternate between two groups of three, and three groups of two, many transcribers prefer to give a combined meter signature. This enables small note values to be beamed according to the metric grouping of each measure. The effect, however, would still be perceived as syncopation.[41]

A popular vihuela piece in which hemiola patterns are prevalent is the setting of *Guárdame las vacas* by Luis de Narváez. (Note that in this tablature, the highest pitched course on the bottom line):

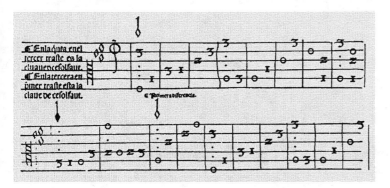

39 For examples of transcriptions using multimetric notation, see Luis Gásser, *Luis Milán on Sixteenth-Century Performance Practice* (Bloomington and Indianapolis: Indiana University Press, 1996); and Jacobs, *Luis de Milán: El Maestro* (University Park and London: Penn. State Univ. Press, 1971).

40 David Grimes, *The Complete Fantasias of Luys Milán* (Pacific, MO: Mel Bay, 2000), xii-xiii.

41 See Frank Koonce, "Rhythm vs. Meter" *Soundboard* 32, Nos. 3-4 (Garden Grove, CA: 2007): 36-43.

In most modern editions, three *compases* are combined to form a modern metrical measure. Some are with a 2:1 reduction and a meter of 6/4.[42]

If a 4:1 reduction is used instead, the transcriber must decide whether the beat subdivisions should be beamed in groups of two or three. In the example below, measures 1, 2, and 4 are beamed in three groups of two—the downbeat and upbeat of each original *compás*. In measure 3, the hemiola grouping of two groups of three is more appropriate because of the rhythmic placement of the bass notes.

Since the original *compás* divisions imply no accent pattern, it is also possible for measures 1 and 2 to be divided as two groups of three.

In summary, while tactus reduction often enables rhythmic structures to be more clearly shown through eighth- and sixteenth-note beaming, a disadvantage is that the transcriber must commit to imposing one particular interpretation when other possibilities may need to be considered [see 8.4].

---

42 See, for instance, Emilio Pujol, *Hispanæ Citharæ Ars Viva* (London: Schott, 1955), 15; and Frederick Noad, *The Renaissance Guitar* (New York: Ariel. 1974), 78-79.

—5—

Theory and Performance Practice

5.1. Modes

European music from the late Middle Ages and Renaissance is organized around eight scale-like structures called "modes." These are sometimes referred to as the "church" or "ecclesiastical" modes, and were called *tonos* (tones) by the Spanish vihuelists. Each is distinguished by its "final" (ending note), its order of half and whole steps, and its "ambitus" (range). The eight modes can be divided into four related pairs, characterized as "authentic" and "plagal," in which each pair shares the same final. If the ambitus of a melody is above the final, it is considered authentic; and if it is both above and below the final, it is plagal. The authentic modes extend one octave above the final, but allow for one added pitch at each end. Because of this, the ambitus can encompass ten notes. The plagal modes extend five pitches above the final and four below, with the added allowance of an extra pitch at each end.[43]

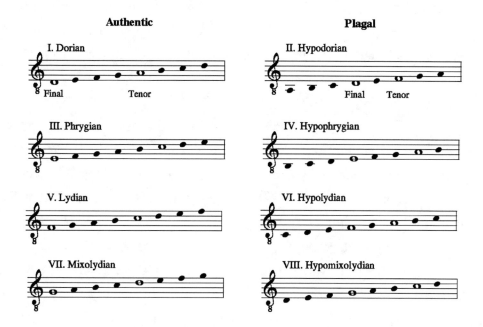

The primary tonal center of each mode is its final. Additionally, emphasis is placed on an important secondary tonal center called the "tenor" or "dominant," sometimes also referred to as the "reciting tone." In the authentic modes, the tenor is a fifth diatonic step above the final, with the exception of mode III in which it is a sixth above. It is a third above the final in the plagal modes II and VI, but a fourth above in IV and VIII. Early theorists usually describe the core distances (D-d, E-e, etc.) of a mode as the combination of a perfect fifth (*diapente*) and a perfect fourth (*diatessaron*) instead of as one octave. This reinforces the tenor as being an important tonal center. Stylized harmonic *cláusulas* (cadences) were developed by the vihuelists on the tonal centers of each mode. These reflect the emerging concept of "goal-directed harmonic gestures" and foreshadow our modern concept of functional harmony.[44]

---

43 Craig H. Russell, "The Eight Modes as Tonal Forces in the Music of Luis Milán," *De Música Hispana et Aliis* I (1990): 323-326. The reader is strongly encouraged to consult this excellent article for detailed information about modal practices in sixteenth-century Spain. The present discussion on modal theory was largely drawn from Russell's explanations. Also see Richard H. Hoppin, *Medieval Music* (New York: W.W. Norton, 1978).

44 Ibid.

According to Craig H. Russell:

> The early sixteenth century saw a metamorphic transformation in the roles that harmony, modality, and tonality played in Western music. The conventions and expectations inherited from Medieval plainchant—particularly with regard to the "Church modes"—were significantly altered as they emerged in the evolving context of Renaissance counterpoint. No longer were vertical harmonies seen as the mere incidental by-product of intertwining contrapuntal lines but were viewed instead as sonorities inherently charged with direction. To the late Renaissance composer, harmonies did more than succeed each other: they actually progressed, one sonority pushing to the next, impelling the composition forward.[45]

5.2. Transposed Modes and "Key" Signatures

A method for identifying notes and for solmization had been developed centuries earlier by the Benedictine monk Guido d'Arezzo. This system, which persisted into the Renaissance, is based on the hexachord—six stepwise notes in which the adjacent pitches are a whole tone apart except for the middle two, which are a semitone apart. These six pitches are named *ut, re, mi, fa, sol,* and *la* (the origin of our current solfeggio system), with the semitone always occurring between *mi* and *fa*.

The lowest line of the music staff, G (two octaves below middle C), was referred to as *Gamma*—the lowest theoretical note in music. Guido assigned *ut* to this line, from which the term *Gamma-ut* (later, *Gamut*) evolved. The second lowest note was called *A re*, the third *B mi*, and so on. According to Guido's system, a hexachord could start on the notes G, C or F, and notes within different octaves could be distinguished from one other. Thus, the second hexachord begins on *c fa ut* (or *cefaut*), the third on *f fa ut* (*fefaut*), and the fourth on *g sol re ut* (*gesolreut*). Hexachords that begin on C are called "natural." Those beginning on G are "hard" because they contain B-natural, and those beginning on F are "soft" because they have a B-flat. As explained in 5.1, scale structures in Renaissance theory were not octave-based as they are today. To the Renaissance musician, a melody larger than one hexachord would require shifting to another hexachord. This is achieved through "mutation," a process in which a pivotal note is assigned the syllable from its position in the new hexachord.

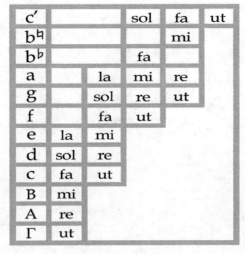

c'			sol	fa	ut
b♮				mi	
b♭			fa		
a		la	mi	re	
g		sol	re	ut	
f		fa	ut		
e	la	mi			
d	sol	re			
c	fa	ut			
B	mi				
A	re				
Γ	ut				

Hexachord Table

45   Ibid., 321

Using Guido's hexachord system, vihuela composers usually provided written directions and sometimes *clave* (clef or "key") signs at the beginning of their tablatures. These enabled players to identify the mode of each piece by locating the position of their semitones on the fingerboard. From the information provided by Narváez for his first fantasia, the player knows that it is in Dorian mode on a vihuela pitched in G, and that its final—as determined by the semitones—is on the second fret of the fifth course.

Primer tono. Por gesolreut.	First mode. In g (*sol re ut*).
En la cuarta en vazio	On the fourth open [course]
está la clave de fefaut.	is the f (*fe fa ut*) clef.
En la tercera en el tercertraste	On the third [course] at the third fret
está la clave de cesolfaut.	is the c' (*ce sol fa ut*) clef.

Narváez was the first vihuelist to also include notational symbols in the tablature for the *claves* of F and C. A three-diamond sign marks the course on which to find F, while a double cross hatch marks that on which to find C. The third symbol shown in the example below is a tempo marking [see 5.3].

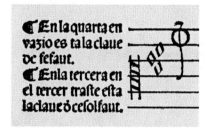

If the player encounters a tablature in which neither mode or clefs is indicated, Bermudo advises: "Look at any of the strings where a semitone is formed, and by it you will know the above mentioned [i.e., mode and clefs]. That is, if a zero occurs on the third string, and next or later a 1 occurs on the said string, then the third string open is *mi*."[46]

Ward notes:

> This theoretical recognition of the divorce of mode and pitch, forced on the vihuelists (and lutenists) by the physical limitations of their instruments, tablature notation, and their illiterate "pupils," must be considered a factor contributing to the break-up of modal theory in the 16th century.[47]

5.3. Tempo

Milán was the first vihuelist to give specific information regarding tempo. He did so through verbal instructions such as:

---

46   Ward, "Vihuela de Mano," 43. Ward cites and translates Bermudo, ch. 72, fol. 100.

47   Ibid., 46.

1. *muy despacio* (very slow)

2. *despacio* (slow)

3. *algo despacio* (somewhat slow)

4. *ni aprisa ni despacio*, and, *ni muy despacio ni muy aprisa sino con un compás bien mesurado* (neither fast nor slow," and, "neither too fast nor too slow, but with a well-measured *compás*)

5. *algo apriessa* (somewhat fast)

6. *aprisa* (fast)

7. *algo apresurado* (somewhat hurried)

8. *compás apresurado o batido* (with a hurried or beaten *compás*)

9. *cuanto más se tañerá con el compás apresurado meor parecerá* (the more it is played with a hurried *compás* the better it will seem)

The word *apresurado* (hurried" or "rushed) is often translated in modern editions as "fast," like *aprisa*. I believe that it is more likely to indicate what we now think of as *tempo rubato*—a modifying of the tempo through accelerations and retardations [see 7.3]. This possibility is reinforced by Milán's instructions in number 8 where he seems to call for either *tempo rubato* "or" a steady beat. For a style of playing he that calls *tañer de gala* (playing gallantly), he unquestionably calls for *rubato* phrasing, as well as changes in the tempo [see 7.2].

Narváez was the first to include notational symbols for tempo, a practice followed by Mudarra and Valderrábano:

Narváez		Mudarra		Valderrábano	
₵	very slow	₵	slow	₵	slow
Ø	somewhat fast	₵	neither fast nor slow	₵	faster
		₵	fast	₵	very much faster

Pisador, Fuenllana, and Daza do not give tempo indications, however, Fuenllana notes: "one must be satisfied with the abilities of his hands."[48] Daza's use of two of the above symbols, which correspond to Mudarra's "fast" and "slow," are the two indications of duple time that were frequently used in the sixteenth century. There is no evidence that these have tempo significance for Daza's music.

5.4. Tuning and Temperament

Vihuelas were fitted with gut frets tied around the neck. Four methods of fret placement are provided by Bermudo, all of which are based on Pythagorean tuning.[49] The Pythagorean system produces pure fifths and fourths, but also produces semitones that are not equal.[50] Therefore, to sixteenth-century musicians "enharmonic" tones such as G-

---

48 ... *sólo quiero dezir, que cada uno se deve conformar con la dispusición de sus manos.*

49 For a thorough discussion of Pythagorean tuning according to the methods of Bermudo, see Maria Therese Annoni, "Tuning, Temperament and Pedagogy for the Vihuela in Juan Bermudo's *Declaracion de Instrumentos Musicales* (1555)," (Ph.D. diss., Ohio State University, 1989).

50 Bermudo's fourth method of tuning introduces modifications to the Pythagorean system that begin to approach equal temperament. Ibid., 157-167.

sharp and A-flat would not be identical. Bermudo distinguishes whether a particular fret must serve as *mi* (flat) or *fa* (sharp) in the mode being played. The *mi* frets are a comma higher than *fa* frets, a difference that is "perceptible to the ear."[51] For this reason, a fret was sometimes adjusted to accommodate the mode of the piece being played. Nevertheless, since one fret served all six courses, any fret placement might still produce undesirable pitches on one or more courses. Bermudo notes that it is possible to compensate for these "missing" (unplayable) tones in different ways. One method (which he personally discourages) is to slant the fret to produce *mi's* on one course and *fa's* on another, as needed. The other ways include: playing the "missing" tone on a different string and fret; using a double fret with two thicknesses, either of which could be selected at will; or pushing or pulling on the note to change the string tension as it is being stopped.[52]

5.5. Playing Technique

Three plucking techniques have been described in some detail for the playing of rapid scale passages, called *pasos* or *redobles* [see 5.7.3]:

> *Dedillo* is a down and up movement of the index finger, so that the tip is used like a plectrum. Fuenllana considered this technique to be unsatisfactory because the string is touched by the flesh on the upward stroke and by the nail on the downward stroke.[53]

> *Dos dedos* is an alternation between the thumb and the index finger. According to Venegas de Henestrosa, *dos dedos* had two variants: *figuets castellana* (Castilian), with the thumb held outside the fingers, and *figueta estranjera* (foreign), with the thumb held inside the fingers, as in Renaissance lute technique.[54]

> The third method is an alternation of the index and middle fingers. Fuenllana and Venegas de Henestrosa both praised this as being the most perfect way of playing.[55]

There is almost no discussion of left-hand technique. According to Griffiths, Venegas de Henestrosa recommends using open strings and comfortable fingering patterns whenever possible.[56] Other early writers such as Bermudo, Fuenllana, and Mudarra recommend sustaining polyphonic voices for their proper values by not lifting fingers too quickly [see 9.3]. Bermudo and Fuenllana also mention that one string of a course may be stopped, while allowing the other to sound at its open pitch, to provide an additional note. Fuenllana indicates that he uses this technique only when necessary to preserve the integrity of complex counterpoint.[57]

---

51 Bermudo, fol. 195, cited in Ward, "Vihuela de mano," 32.

52 Ibid., 33-34.

53 This comment also infers that some vihuelists played with nails while others did not.

54 Venegas de Henestrosa, 159-60.

55 Ibid.

56 John Griffiths, "The vihuela: performance practice, style, and context," in Victor Anand Coelho, ed., *Performance on Lute, Guitar, and Vihuela: Historical Practice and Modern Interpretation* (Cambridge: Cambridge University Press, 1997), 173-174.

57 Fuenllana, fols. iv, v-v^r, cited in Griffiths, "vihuela: performance practice," 175.

5.6. Repertoire genres

5.6.1. Fantasía (fantasy; fantasia) is the name frequently given to pieces that are free and improvisatory-sounding and that, according to Milán, "proceed from the imagination and industry of their author." The term was often used synonymously with *ricercar* and *tiento* [see 5.6.2]. The most common type of fantasia is built from numerous sections—each based on a single theme or idea and linked together into a homogenous, tonally coherent whole—moving forward by means of some abstract narrative impulse. In this sense, fantasias have similar structure to renaissance madrigals and motets, but without text. As well as this kind of polythematic fantasia, it is possible to define several other fantasia sub-categories according to composition techniques that are used.[58] The vihuela repertory includes a number of monothematic fantasias in which a single theme is used throughout, often by using a predetermined cantus firmus as an ostinato. Another type is the "parody fantasia", favored extensively by Valderrábano, that borrows thematic material from another work, usually from vocal polyphony but sometimes also from other instrumental works. In these works, the vihuelist would take all or part of a polyphonic vocal work such as a mass, motet, or madrigal, and re-work it into an instrumental solo [see 5.6.3].

5.6.2. Tiento is a term derived from *tentar* (to test; to try out). Among the vihuelists, it was first used by Milán in the plural Portuguese spelling, *tentos*. For Milán, it signified an improvisatory-sounding piece with the same essential characteristics as a fantasia. The later tientos of Mudarra and Fuenllana are shorter and more homophonic than those of Milán. Mudarra used his tientos like brief preludes to introduce groups of pieces organized by mode, while Fuenllana's are similar in nature but are presented as a group, one in each of the eight modes.

5.6.3. Intabulation is the term for a tablature arrangement of a vocal work that originally was in mensural notation. Beginning with Narváez, all of the vihuela publications contain many intabulations of polyphonic works by Franco-Flemish composers such as Josquin and Gombert. Ward distinguishes three procedures: strict intabulation (which may include some ornamentation), the use of *glosas* [see 5.7.3], and parody or "parody by means of paraphrase" [see 5.6.1].[59] These compositions make up just over two thirds of the surviving repertory and obviously had an important didactic value as well as being used simply for recreational listening. The intabulation was the way in which many instrumentalists learned the techniques of vocal composition that they later applied to their own composition.

5.6.4. Diferencias. Narváez is the first known composer to write instrumental pieces identified as being sets of variations, referred to as *diferencias*. The term and practice possibly evolved from a vocal tradition of improvising "differences" on the repetitive chord patterns used for accompanying the texts of long *romances* [see 5.6.6.1]. Indeed, most instrumental *diferencias* follow the harmonic progressions of popular *romance* accompaniments, and names such as *Guárdame las vacas* and *Conde Claros* refer to the *romances* with which the patterns were customarily associated.

---

58 See Ward, "The Vihuela de mano," or Griffiths, "The Vihuela Fantasia."

59 John M. Ward, "The Use of Borrowed Material in 16th-Century Instrumental Music," *Journal of the American Musicological Society* 5 (Summer 1952): 88-98.

5.6.5. Pavana. According to Milán and a few other sources, the *pavana* was introduced into Spain from Italy. The word is believed to come from "Pava," which refers to the northern town of Padua in local dialect. Dance and music in the Paduan style are described as *alla pavana*. Some later sources suggest a possible Spanish etymology from the word *pavón*, "peacock."[60] The *pavana* was a stately court dance in slow to moderate tempo that often was in the form of a processional. In Italy, but not in Spain, it frequently was followed by one of the faster dances such as the *gagliarda*, *saltarello*, or *piva*. Although meter was not yet reflected in tablature notation, *pavanas* are usually transcribed in simple duple meter. A few, however, such as the sixth one by Milán, are in triple meter.

5.6.6. Works for Voice and Vihuela.

In most vocal pieces with vihuela accompaniment, one voice of the vihuela doubles the vocal part. This voice is usually written as part of the tablature and distinguished by the use of red ink or by placing marks (*puntillos*) next to their ciphers. In some vocal works, the voice part is written on a separate staff in mensural notation above the tablature.

>   **5.6.6.1. Romance.** The *romance* is a dramatic ballad that was often set to music and whose themes, in general, concern "the Carolingian epics, the history of the re-conquest of Spain by the Christians against the Moors, Biblical subjects, novels of chivalry and finally, those which were called 'new romances', concerned the wars in Granada (the last stronghold of the Moors) waged by the Catholic Kings."[61] They are of significant importance because they are the main source of information about the early historical events in Spain. In the sixteenth century, Spanish poets and musicians often wrote new verses, or *glosas*, that were added to the older medieval themes. Specific melodies (*tonadas*) and/or harmonic progressions became associated with the singing of certain *romances* and became a basis for improvisation and composed sets of instrumental variations [see 5.6.4].
>
>   Many *romances* survive in different versions in sixteenth-century songbooks called *cancioneros*. Two of the earliest are *Cancionero de la Colombina* (ca. 1490) and the Cancionero de Palacio (c. 1500). The first major collection of romance texts was published as the *Cancionero General* (1511). Many other poetic collections followed during the sixteenth century, including the *Cancionero de Romances* (ca. 1547) and the *Silva de Romances* (1550-51).
>
>   **5.6.6.2. Villancico.** The *villancico*, which is related to *villano* (peasant), is a rustic or popular song. It is usually lighter than the *romance*, with poetic texts about love or other popular themes. A *villancico* consists of several *coplas* (stanzas) in two sections, the *mudanza* and the *vuelta* (or *buelta*). The form is usually ABBAA, or abbreviated to ABBA.
>
>   **5.6.6.3. Soneto** (sonnet). Research by Ignacio Navarrete has shown that most of the vihuela *sonetos* are settings of hendecasyllabic poems (those with eleven syllables to a line of verse), whether ac-

---

60 See Maurice Esses, *Dance and instrumental Diferencias in Spain During the 17ᵗʰ and 18ᵗʰ Centuries* (Stuyvesant, NY: Pendragon Press), vol. 1, 692.

61 Rodrigo de Zayas, Slipcase notes of the Musical Heritage Society, No. 3208, *Spanish Vihuelists of the 16th Century, History of Spanish Music*, vol. 16.

tual literary sonnets or not.[62] The exception to this practice is Valderrábano, who wrote twenty-two instrumental works that he labeled as *sonetos*. It appears that he was using the term imprecisely, perhaps simply to indicate a tune that was known to him [see 10.3].

5.7. Ornamentation and Embellishment[63]

5.7.1. **Quiebro (quiebros)**, from *quebrar* (to break), is the Spanish term that was often used for a short ornament applied to a single note. While the vihuela tablatures employ no signs to indicate decoration of individual notes, there is contemporary evidence from keyboard sources that such ornaments were employed. In his important keyboard treatise, Tomás de Santa Maria writes that the *quiebro* involves the main note and either its upper or lower neighbor tone, and that it may be *sencillo* (simple)—with one alternation, or *reiterado* (repeated).[64] Today, English-speaking musicians usually distinguish these as two separate ornaments: the "trill"—an alternation between the main note and its upper neighbor, and the "mordent"—an alternation between the main note and its lower neighbor.

In another important treatise for keyboard, harp and vihuela, Luis Venegas de Henestrosa writes that the *quiebro* on a stringed instrument is "rocking (*menear*) the finger on the string and fret that you wish to touch; or, holding it in that place, trilling (*quebrar*) with the second or third fingers, one fret or two above, etc."[65]

The first method identified by Venegas appears to be what we now think of as vibrato. However, this probably would have been a more intense "shake" of the hand on a single note to give an effect similar to that of a trill or mordent—not as a general component of tone production.

5.7.2. Redoble (redobles). According to Santa Maria, the redoble is a four-note turn that encompasses the main note and that consists of a whole tone and a semitone. He notes that, on long notes, the *redoble* could be followed by a *quiebro reiterado*.

The vihuelists used the term in a more generalized way, however, for any kind of fast passagework in which longer note values are "redoubled" [see 5.7.3].

---

62 Ignacio Navarrete, "The Problem of the *Soneto* in the Spanish Renaissance Vihuela Books," *Sixteenth Century Journal*, vol. 23, No. 4 (Winter, 1992): 769-789.

63 I use the term "ornamentation" for figurations that emphasize a single note, and "embellishment" for diminutions (small-value subdivisions) that are connective—leading from one important beat to another.

64 Tomás de Santa Maria: Libro *llamado Arte de tañer fantasia, assi par Tecla como vihuela, y todo instrumeto...* (Valladolid, 1565); facsimile with English trans. by Almonte C. Howell Jr. and Warren E. Hultberg, 2 vols. (Pittsburgh: Latin American Literary Review Press, 1991); cited in Nelly van Ree Bernard, Interpretation of 16th-Century Iberian Music on the Clavichord (Buren, The Netherlands: Frits Knuf Publishers, 1989), 35.

65 Venegas de Henestrosa, 159.

5.7.3. Glosa (glosas) refers to diminution—a variation technique in which notes of a melody are divided into small figurations. Frequently, works originally composed for vocal ensembles were glossed in order to transform them into idiomatic instrumental music. This seldom happens in vihuela music because, as Fuenllana observes, the resulting texture of an unembellished intabulation is already difficult enough to play without adding a further layer of embellishment. The best-known work of this type for vihuela is a *glosa* by Fuenllana that follows his intabulation of the French chanson *Tant que vivray* [see 12.3]. The term is also used interchangeably with *redobles* and *pasos* [see 5.7.2], and some more extended and elaborate *glosas* could also be considered as melodic *diferencias* [see 5.6.3]. Mudarra included five compositions that he called *glosas* but, as pointed out by Ward, these are really parody fantasies [see 5.6.1].[66]

With regard to intabulations of polyphonic works, the appropriateness of adding *glosas* is called into question. Ward notes that there was a connection between the vihuela intabulations and their contemporary vocal models. Those of the Josquin generation, in which paired imitation was common, have more embellishment. Later works with thicker textures, such as those of Gombert and Morales, leave less room for embellishment.[67] A comment in Valderrábano's publication of 1547 supports this observation:

> [I] did not put glosas in all of the compositions so that they can be played better and with less difficulty; and each one may glosa according to his hand because the music which is now composed carries so much counterpoint that it does not allow glosas; however, in some [compositions] I placed what was convenient as a pattern for those who might wish to play it [the glosa].[68]

Fuenllana expresses concern about inappropriate embellishments except "at cadences or at such time as the composition gives the place." He writes:

> I do not add glosses at every opportunity in composed works, because I am of the opinion that embellishments and ornaments should not be used to hide the truth of the composition, as we see when some players, content with their own opinion alone, compose all over again works that very good composers have crafted with excellent artifice and good spirit, but when left to them become enshrouded with all kinds of embellishments, governed entirely by their own caprice.[69]

Bermudo, the harshest critic of overused glosas, writes that "importune glosas" are "the greatest corruption and damage to music."[70] Such comments suggest that embellishments were commonly practiced by vihuelists, but perhaps too often by players who lacked the skill to do them well.

---

66 Ward, "Vihuela de Mano," 86.

67 Ibid., 215.

68 Valderrábano, fol. 3, trans. Ward, "Vihuela de Mano." 93.

69 Fuenllana, fol. v, trans. John Griffiths, "How to Play the Vihuela According to Juan Bermudo, Vocal Polyphony and Instrumental Tablature," http://www.rmguitar.info/vTutor.htm (accessed 8 May 2007), 11. This is the English translation of the Introduction to *Tañer Vihuela Según Juan Bermudo: Polifonía Vocal y Tablaturas Instrumentales*, (Zargoza: Institución 'Fernando El Católico', 2003).

70 Bermudo, fol 29ᵛ, trans. Ward, "Vihuela de Mano." 93.

—6—
Editorial Procedures

This is not an *urtext* or critical edition, but a performance edition for the modern guitar. As explained in the Preface, I have made subjective choices that reflect my personal interpretive and technical preferences. Facsimiles of some of the original tablatures are provided for comparison. For access to images of the other tablatures, the reader is directed to the publications referenced in 1.3 and 1.5.

I assigned meters that are larger than the original compás only to those pieces whose accent patterns fall naturally into predictable larger groupings. For pieces that otherwise would require many metric changes, I settled on keeping the barlines between each *compás* as in the original tablature. This way, as explained by theorist Paul Creston, the barline remains a "useful servant" and fulfills the function of rhythm as "ordered movement."[71] The player may wish to draw phrase markings to clarify rhythmic groupings that cross over barlines [see 4.4–4.6].

Sharp and flat signs placed at the beginning of staff lines in my transcriptions should not be thought of as modern key signatures for determining the modality or tonality of a piece. They are used only to avoid clutter by minimizing the need for written accidentals in the score.

My suggested fingerings require the modern guitar to be tuned to the same intervallic patterns as on the original instruments. Six-course vihuela pieces will require lowering the third string a semitone from G to F sharp, while five-course vihuela pieces and four-course guitar pieces correspond to modern guitar tuning. A capo may be used, if desired, to replicate the nominal tunings of the original instruments.

For transcriptions of parody fantasias and other intabulations of existing polyphony, I studied their vocal models whenever possible to determine voicing. As explained in 4.2, the durational values of notes in some voices are not always apparent from the tablature. Because of this ambiguity, my choices are interpretive. Even when original durations could be determined, I sometimes chose to hold notes longer than indicated for musical or technical reasons. I believe this is justified because the lighter, gut-strung vihuela is more "forgiving" than the modern guitar with regard to articulations and textures. Also, my suggested fingerings do not exclusively follow the original fret and string indications of the tablature. I made some changes because of the larger size of the modern guitar. I made other changes when the original positions seemed unnecessarily awkward. Perhaps some of these had been chosen for intonation concerns that no longer apply to an instrument in equal temperament [see 5.4]. Again, given the ambiguities of tablature notation and the subjectivity associated with transcriptions, I believe that players should always consult the tablature for an unfiltered look at the original music and for the experience of determining their own solutions.

---

71 Paul Creston, *Principles of Rhythm* (New York: Franco Colombo, 1964), 100.

6.1. Editorial Guitar Notation

③   An encircled numeral designates the string on which a note is to be played.

IV₄ ⌐   A Roman numeral indicates a *barré* at the designated fret. An Arabic numeral to its right specifies the minimum number of strings to be covered at that fret. A horizontal "line of continuation" shows the duration of the *barré*.

IV₄ ---⌐   A "hinge" *barré*, in which either the tip or base segment of the first finger is lifted off the strings, is indicated when all or part of the line of continuation is dotted.

A left bracket encompassing two notes indicates a double stop (two notes stopped by the first finger of the left hand).

A note within brackets is a suggested addition to that which is given in the tablature.

A note within parentheses is a suggested omission from that which is given in the tablature.

A small open-ended slur to the right of a note means that it may be sustained for longer than indicated. It is also used to show a tie or a suspension that cannot be fully realized on the guitar with the given fingering.

6.2. Presentation of Spanish Texts

For the purposes of this edition, Spanish texts with archaic spellings involving b versus v, j and g, u and v, f and s, and so on, have been regularized according to modern usage. Singers who wish to replicate historical pronunciation should refer to the original spellings found in the tablature and seek out resource materials that address this complicated subject.[72] Abbreviations have been replaced by complete spellings. Punctuations, accents, capital letters, and word divisions have also been adjusted to conform to modern practices.

The text underlay in tablatures is not aligned with the rhythm of the music; therefore, their musical placement is subject to many interpretations. My choices are based on my preferences, with the intent of placing accented syllables on strong beats of the music. The reader is encouraged to consider alternatives. Slurs written below the text indicate vowel sounds that should be elided.

---

72 For instance, see Timothy J. McGee, A.G. Rigg, and David N. Klausner, *Singing Early Music: The Pronunciation of European Languages in the Late Middle Ages and Renaissance* (Bloomington: Indiana University Press, 1996); also J. Donald Bowen and Robert P. Stockwell, *Patterns of Spanish Pronunciation: A Drillbook* (Chicago: Chicago University Press, 1960).

–7–

Luis Milán

Luis (Luys) Milán (ca. 1506-1559) was a writer and poet as well as a musician. He was also a nobleman associated with the Valencian court of Germaine de Foix and Fernando de Aragón. The second of his three books, *Libro de música de vihuela de mano intitulado el maestro* is believed to be the first collection of instrumental music ever published in Spain.[73] It had been submitted to the printer in 1535 but was not released until the end of 1536. As indicated by the title, *El Maestro* (The Teacher), it also serves a didactic purpose with its seventy-two pieces arranged in a progressive order of difficulty. Included are instrumental works—forty fantasias, four *tentos*, and six *pavanas*—and accompanied songs in various languages—twelve *villancicos*, four *romances*, and six *sonetos*.

According to Griffiths:

> [Milán] is unlikely to have had a formal musical training in counterpoint and vocal polyphony, instead he was an improviser probably descended from an older unwritten musical tradition of instrumentalist singers. Milán himself tells us that the works in *El Maestro* were all composed on the vihuela and then written down, making them, in effect, transcriptions of his own improvisations. Understanding him as singer of *romances*, as a musical storyteller, provides enormous insight in performing his music: in discovering the narrative logic within his *fantasías*, and in performing his music today as if we were the original improvisers.[74]

Milán's tablature is different from that of the other known vihuelists in that he used the highest line of the staff to represent the highest course (as in Neapolitan and French lute tablatures). Most significantly, he was the first composer—for any instrument—to give specific information regarding tempo, through descriptive instructions, and the first to describe what we now think of as *tempo rubato* [see 5.3 and 7.2].

His fantasias have "textures that usually evoke an imitative style, but they are most frequently crafted as pseudo-imitation, built from short, accompanied melodic units that are reiterated at different pitches or in sequences to create the illusion of an imitative texture."[75] Most may be described as multimetric, with freely flowing phrase rhythms that would result in many metric changes if transcribed into modern measures that include more than the original *compás* [see 4.6].

7.1. Fantasías 1 and 3. Both of these pieces are in the *primer tono* (first mode), which Milán composed imagining his vihuela to be tuned in A [see 3.1]. On the modern guitar (pitched in E) this transposed mode becomes A-B-C-D-E-F♯-G-A.

73 Milán's first book (1535), *Libro de Motes de damas y cavalleros Intitulado El juego de mandar*, describes a popular parlor game. His third book, *El Cortesano* (1561) is a valuable source of information about court life in Valencia and musical practices of the time. See Lluís del Milà (Luis Milán), El *Cortesano*. ed. Antonio Tordera and Vicent-Josep Escartí (Valencia: Universitat de Valencia, 2001), 2 vols.

74 Griffiths, "The Two Renaissances," 4.

75 John Griffiths, "Milán, Luys," *The New Grove Dictionary of Music and Musicians,* 2nd. ed., vol. 16, ed. Stanley Sadie (London: Macmillan, 2001), 669.

Milán provides these instructions:

> This first fantasia that is notated below is in the first mode, and the more it is played on the vihuela with the hurried *compás* [see 5.3 and 7.2], the better will he seem who plays within the terms (*terminos*) in which this fantasia moves: playing in the first mode. Observe this fantasia well to see what cadences it makes, its placement, and where it ends, for in this way one can see all that can be done in the first mode.[76]

For the third fantasia, he writes:

> The fantasia written below is in the first mode and also is to be played with the *compás* somewhat hurried, and is placed on the vihuela in the same way as the previous two fantasias. The book gives you these three fantasias in the first mode and all placed on the vihuela in the same way because they use the easy parts [of the fingerboard] as I have already told you.[77]

7.2. Fantasías 10, 11, and 16 are works of *consonancias y redobles*, chord sections that alternate with running scale passages. Milán calls for the runs to be fast and the chords slow:

> The fantasias of these present fourth and fifth books [into] which we are now entering, present music that is like one getting to know the vihuela through *consonancias* mixed with *redobles*, which is commonly called "playing *dedillo*" [see 5.5.1]. To play [this music] with its natural spirit you must guide yourself in this way: play all the *consonancias* with the *compás* slow, and the *redobles* with the *compás* fast, and pause a little at each fermata (*coronado*). This is the music that I said, in the contents of the present volume, that you would find in the fourth and fifth sections that has more with respect to playing gallantly (*tañer de gala*) than much [other] music or [than with keeping the] beat. And these two following fantasias move through the ambitus of the first and second modes.[78]

7.3. Pavanas 2, 4, 6. Milán identifies all of his solo pieces, including these *pavanas*, as "fantasias" because they "proceed from the imagination and industry of their author:"

---

76 *Esta primera fantasia que aqui debaxo esta figurado es del primero tono, y quanto mas se tañera con el compas apressurado mejor parecera el que tañera en la vihuela por los terminos que esta fantasia anda: tañe por el primero tono. Miren bien la dicha fantasia que clausulas haze; y que terminos tiene: y de donde fenece: porque en ella veran todo lo que justamente el primero tono puede hazer.* (I have translated the word "terminos" to mean ambitus or range, as recommended by Russell [see 5.1.1] and also to refer to the placement of the music on the vihuela. In this fantasia, for example, the first mode is placed on the vihuela so that the final is on the open fifth course, irrespective of the sounding pitch of the instrument.)

77 *Esta fantasia que aqui debaxo esta escrita es del primero tono y tambien se ha de tañer con el compás algo apressurado y va por los terminos en la vihuela que andan las dos fantasías passadas. Estas tres fantasías por el primero tono y por un mesmo termino hos da el libro porque van por partes faciles como ya he dicho.*

78 *Las fantasias destos presentes cuatro y quinto quadernos que agora entramos: muestran una música la qual es como un tentar la vihuela a consonancias mescladas con redobles que vulgarmente dizen para hazer dedillo. y para tañerla con su natural ayre haueys os de regir desta manera. Todo lo que sera consonancias tañerlas con el compás a espacio y todo lo que sera redobles tañerlos con el compás apriessa. y parar de tañer en cada coronado un poco. Esta es la música que en la tabla del presente libro dixe que hallariedes en el cuatro y quinto quadernos que tiene mas respecto a tañer de gala que de mucha música ni compas: Y estas dos fantasias siguientes van por los terminos del primero y segundo tono.*

These six fantasias that follow, as I told you above, are similar in their spirit and style to the same *pavanas* that are played in Italy; and since they imitate them, we may call them *pavanas*. The first four were invented by me. The melody (*sonada*) of the two that then follow was made in Italy and the setting is mine. They should be played with the *compás* somewhat hurried and must be played two or three times.[79]

Today, Milan's six *pavanas* are among the best-known pieces from the vihuela repertoire. They are deceptively simple when transcribed into modern notation and with fingerings in modern-guitar tuning. Because of this, they are found in countless guitar method books and anthologies. However, much more can be learned by the advanced student who is able to reconsider these pieces from a stylistic perspective, especially through an understanding of the intricacies of Milan's multimetric rhythmic phrase rhythms and through experiencing the original tuning and fingering positions.[80]

When using the original fingerings, it will become apparent that certain chords cannot be sustained in the manner to which we are accustomed. For example, see those in measures 11 and 14 of *Pavana 2* (mm. 1 and 4 of the excerpt below).

Most players are tempted to re-finger passages such as these. However, we must try to understand the reasons for Milan's choices and ask ourselves why he too was not bothered by these seemingly abrupt chord detachments. I believe the answer lies in the improvisatory nature of Milan's music and the likelihood that he played with *rubato* and ample spaciousness between the large gestures of his phrase groupings. For example, the downbeat of measure 11 can be played *tenuto* (held a little longer), and even more so if some degree of acceleration has taken place in measures 9-10. When played this way, there is flexibility in the phrasing of rhythmic structures and there are no abrupt detachments. Although the general perception today is that the pavan should be a slow dance, we must remember that he stresses they should be played with a "hurried" *compás*. This is because each measure of the tablature corresponds with one step of the dance, not two.

The instructions provided for the three *pavanas* in the present collection are:

> This [second] *pavana* that follows goes through the ambitus of the third and fourth mode: and as I already said, it must be played with the *compás* somewhat hurried.[81]

---

79 *Estas seys fantasias que se siguen como arriba hos dixe parescen en su ayre y compostura a las mesmas pavanas que en Italia se tañen: y pues en todo remedan a ellas digamos les pavanas; las quatro primeras son inventadas por mi; las dos que despues se siguen la sonada dellas se hizo en Italia; y la compostura sobre la sonada dellas es mia. Devense tañer con el compás algo apressurado: y requieren tañerse dos o tres vezes.*

80 To mitigate the difficulty of large stretches, a capo may be used if desired.

81 *Esta pavana que se sigue anda por los terminos del tercero y cuatro tono: y como ya he dicho han se de tañer con el compás algo apressurado.*

The [fourth] *pavana* that follows goes through the ambitus of the seventh and eighth mode.[82]

This [sixth] *pavana* is in the proportion of three semibreves per *compás*: and it goes through the ambitus of the previous *pavana,* and all the breves that appear alone [in a *compás*] now have the value of a *compás*.[83]

7.4. Durandarte is possibly the most famous of all the Spanish *romances* [see 5.6.6.1]. Originally the name of Roland's sword, Durandarte also came to refer to the knight himself. Milán adapted a small section of the text, a dialog between Durandarte and Lady Belerma, and set it to music. The voice line is doubled by the vihuela as an inner voice of the four-part texture. Below is a translation of the text:

—Durandarte, Durandarte, good proven knight,
You must remember that happy time now past,
When in finery and with clever inventions,
You proclaimed your love to me.
Now, stranger, tell why you have forgotten me.

—Such words are flattering, lady, from one of your station,
But if I have changed, you have caused me to do so.
For you loved Gaiferos when I was in exile,
And to not suffer offense I shall die despairing.

---

82 *Esta pavana que se sigue anda por los terminos del septimo y octavo tono.*

83 *Esta pavana es a propporcion de tres semibreves compás. y va por los terminos de la pavana passada y todo los breves que hallareys solos valgan agora un compás.* (Note: These are the rhythmic characteristics of a galliard.)

Fantasía 1

Luis Milán

36

Fantasía 3

Luis Milán

38

39

Fantasía 10

Luis Milán

40

41

Fantasía 11

Luis Milán

Fantasía 16

Luis Milán

44

45

Pavana 2

(Fantasía 24)

Luis Milán

Pavana 4

(Fantasía 26)

Luis Milán

48

Pavana 6

(Fantasía 28)

Luis Milán

49

Durandarte

Romance

Luis Milán

a - cor - - - - dár - se - - te de - berí -
A - ho - - - - ra des - co - no - ci - -

a,
do.
dea - - - quel
di por - - -

buen_____ tiem - po pas_____ sa - - - - - -
qué_____ me has ol - vi - da - - - - -

do,
do.

Segunda parte

48

Pa - la -
pues a -

55

bras son - - li - son - je - - ras, se - -
mas - - tes a Gai - fe - - - ros cuan -

61

ño - - ra, de - - vues - tro gra - - do,
do yo fu - i de - ster - ra - - do,

67

que si yo mu - - dan - - sa
y por no suf - - - rir - - ul -

53

Plate 10

Orpheus playing a vihuela

The frontispiece of Milán's *El Maestro*

According to classical Greek mythology, Orpheus—the son of Apollo, the god
of music—was the most accomplished musician in the ancient world.
It was said that when Orpheus played his lyre he was able to tame wild
animals and to cause stones and trees to follow him.

Plate 11

The frontispiece of Narvaez's *Los seys libros del delphín*.
The title refers to the legend of the Greek poet Arion of Methymna who was
saved from drowning by a dolphin that had been charmed by his music.

54

Luis de Narváez

Luis (Luys) de Narváez was born in Granada (date unknown) and is thought to have served there as vihuelist to Francisco de los Cobos, secretary to Emperor Charles V, perhaps as early as 1526. It is likely that he followed his patron to Valladolid where he remained until 1547. By 1548, he was employed as *maestro de los mochachos cantorcicos* (teacher of the choirboys) at the royal chapel of Prince Philip, who later became Philip II, the first King of Spain.[84]

Written accounts indicate that Narváez was an exceptional performer. An especially well-known anecdote attesting to his abilities was written by the royal councilor Luis Zapata (grandson of the dedicatee of Mudarra's *Tres libros de música*):

> There was in Valladolid in my youth, a vihuelist named Narváez, of such extraordinary skill, that upon four parts in mensural music in a book, he improvised on the vihuela another four, a thing miraculous to those who did not understand music, and to those who did understood it, most miraculous.[85]

With the exception of two motets published in France, all of Narváez's music is found in one publication entitled *Los seys libros del delphín de música de cifras para tañer vihuela* (The six books of the dolphin), published 1538.[86] Included are fourteen fantasias, intabulations of five mass movements by Josquin and four French *chansons*, one dance setting, seven variation sets, and seven accompanied songs (two *romances* and five *villancicos*).

According to Griffiths:

> It is likely that [Narváez] met Francesco da Milano in Rome while there with Francisco de los Cobos, and that this was influential in the development of a new style of vihuela fantasia which he proudly claims to have introduced into Spain. This new imitative fantasia rapidly became the predominant style and prevailed for the following fifty years at least. These fantasias derive from the same techniques used by composers of motets and masses, and are conceived as though the vihuela were an ensemble of three or four contrapuntal voices, but blending abstract polyphonic ideas with the idiomatic devices suggested intuitively by the vihuela. Other works by Narváez, however, also show links to Milán and earlier improvised traditions, especially his *diferencias* or variations on the formulas associated with the recitation of *romances* and in improvisations.[87]

---

84 Hopkinson Smith and John Griffiths, "Narváez, Luys de," *New Grove*, vol. 17, 644.

85 Luis Zapata de Chávez, *Miscelanea* (ca. 1592), 61: *De una habilidad de un músico*, trans. Antonio Carona-Alcalde, "The Fernández de Córdoba Printers and the Vihuela Books from Valladolid" (*Lute Society of America Quarterly*, May 2005): 21.

86 Narváez was known abroad. Some of his fantasias were reprinted in France and the Low Countries by Morlaye and Phalèse.

87 Griffiths, "The two Renaissances," 5.

Narváez is the first composer to include symbols indicating tempo [see 5.3], and the first, of any instrument, to include pieces clearly identified as being sets of variations—called *diferencias* [see 5.6.4].

8.1. Fantasía 14. The original title, which appears only in the index table at the end of the second *libro*, is *Otra fantasia del primer Tono* (Another fantasia of the first Mode). On the modern guitar this transposed mode is A, B, C, D, E, F♯, G, A. I changed the first note in measure 27 from C♯ (which I believe is a mistake) to C natural.

Griffiths notes:

> The structure of this short work is typical of the formal architecture of the genre: two imitative episodes of 13 bars (subdivided 8 + 5), plus a "*final*" or brief coda. In the first part, the themes are typical of vocal music, while in the second they are derived more from idiomatic scale figures. The coda is possibly one of those *finales* that vihuelists used to memorize in order for them to be at their immediate disposal for concluding fantasia improvisations. A miniature of transparent texture, this fantasia unfolds with ease and clear artistic direction.[88]

8.2. Canción de Nicolas Gombert. Narváez's original title of this intabulation is *Cancion del primer Tono* (Song or *Chanson* in the first Mode). Narváez does not identify Gombert as the author until the table of contents at the end of the third *libro*, fol. 48ʳ. On the downbeat of measure 44, the original tablature shows B in unison on both the second and third course.

8.3. Mille Regretz (spelled *Mille regres* by Narváez) is one of the best-known works for vihuela. It is an intabulation of a secular Franco-Flemish part song, entitled *Mille regretz de vous habandonner*, which traditionally has been attributed to Josquin des Prez. Evidence suggests, however, that the composer may have been Jean Lemaire de Belges.[89] The original French text and a translation are shown below:

> *Mille regretz de vous habandonne*
> *et d'eslonger vostre fache amoureuse.*
> *Jay si grand dueil et paine douloureuse,*
> *quon me verra brief mes jours definer.*

> A thousand regrets at deserting you
> and leaving behind your loving face.
> I feel so much sadness and such painful distress,
> that it seems to me my days will soon dwindle away.[90]

88 John Griffiths, "How To Play the Vihuela According to Juan Bermudo," 13.

89 See Louise Litterick, *The Josquin Companion*, ed. Richard Sherr (Oxford University Press: Oxford, 2000), 374-75; and David Fallows, "Who composed Mille regretz?," Barbara Haggh, ed., *Essays on Music and Culture in Honor of Herbert Kellman* (Paris, 2001), 214-52.

90 Josquin des Prez, "Mille regretz," *Norton Anthology of Western Music,* 2ⁿᵈ edition, edited by Claude Palisca (New York: W. W. Norton, 1980): 1:228.

Narváez referred to his intabulation as the "Song of the Emperor" because it was said to have been a favorite of the Holy Roman Emperor Charles V. The text preceding the tablature reads, *En la quinta en el tercer traste esta la clave de fefaut. En la tercera e el primer traste esta la clave de solfaut* (On the fifth course, third fret, is the key of F fa ut. On the third course first fret is the key of C sol fa ut.) It can be determined from this information that the final is on the second fret of the fifth course—B on the modern guitar—and that it is in Phrygian mode [see 5.2]. The setting by Narváez is both an intabulation and a *glosa* because, through continuous use of diminution, he changes the character of the piece with abstract figuration.[91]

8.4. Guárdame las vacas was a popular *villancico* theme used by many poets and musicians. It has a four-line refrain that is similar in all surviving texts:[92]

> *Guárdame las vacas,*
> *Carillo, y besarte hé.*
> *Si no, besame tu a mi,*
> *que yo las guardaré.*

> Look after the cows for me,
> Carillo, and I will have to give you a kiss
> If not, kiss me,
> and I will look after them for you.

The theme was also known in England as "The Sheepheard Carillo his Song." It was first published in 1600 in an anthology of Elizabethan poems called *England's Helicon*. The English poetic text is:

> I pre-thee keepe my kine for me
> Carillo, wilt thou? Tell.
> First let me have a kiss of thee,
> And I will keep them well.[93]

Guárdame las vacas was associated with a specific melodic-harmonic formula, known by the same name as the song in Spain, but which in Italy was called the *romanesca*. It consists of a discant melody built on a descending tetrachord (four diatonic tones encompassing the interval of a perfect fourth) over a ground bass pattern of III – VII – i – V / III – VII – i – V - i. However, modern scholars have tended to identify the *romanesca* by the bass pattern alone, while overlooking the discant. Ward notes that instrumental sources can be misleading in this regard because the discant tunes of pieces such as the *romanesca*, *folía*, and *passamezzo* are usually imbedded in elaborate figuration, thus their bass patterns appear to be the constant element:

---

91 Ward, "Borrowed Material," 90-91.

92 An account of all the known versions is found in José Romeu Figueras, "El toro, ensalada poetico-musical inedita. Estudio sobre temas taurinos y vaqueros en la lírica tradicional," *Anuario Musical* 20 (1965): 52-56.

93 Gilbert Chase, *The Music of Spain*, 2nd edition (New York: Dover Publications, 1959), 59.

Because [in the tablature by Narváez] only one note of the discant tune appears in each group of three semibreve *compases* (= one 3/4 measure), the melody, though often lost in figuration, forms the "skeleton" on which such figuration was conceived. The bass pattern, one note of which occurs with each note of the discant tune, determines the harmonies of each variation. This harmonic *ostinato*, a sequence of chords as memorable now as it obviously was in the 16th century, is the distinguishing feature of all settings of the *romanesca*.[94]

When reconstructed with the discant melody, the double structure of the *romanesca* becomes clear:

As explained by Ward, in modern editions of this piece, three binary *compases* are usually assimilated into one measure. However, the rhythmic divisions within each measure often vary from one transcription to another. This is because in some places it is difficult to know whether the intended divisions should be in three groups of two (3/4 meter) or two groups of three (6/8 meter) since both often work well [see 4.7]. In his 1577 publication *De Música Libri Septem*, Francisco de Salinas provides an incipit of the discant melody and rhythm that initially seems to support using 6/8.[95]

Salinas also tells us that the overall structure is hypercatalectic trimeter (three metric feet plus one extra syllable, which equals one four-bar phrase), and he gives the first line of the text: *Guárdame las vacas Carillejo y besar té*. ("Carillo" and "Carillejo" are alternative names; however, only the latter version provides proper accentuation between music and text. The last syllable *té* is a contraction of *te* and *hé*.) The relationship between the music and text is problematic in that Salinas gives us only thirteen notes to accommodate fourteen syllables. The text can be made to fit the rhythm by slurring *lle-jo* on the downbeat of measure three; however, the syllable *sar*, in *besar*, then falls unnaturally on a weak beat of the music. (The stressed syllables should be: GUÁR-da-me las VA-cas Ca-ri-LLE-jo y be-SAR té.) If the placement of this syllable is adjusted to correctly fall on a strong beat, then there are two syllables after the third metric foot.[96]

Guár - da - me   las   va - cas, Ca - ri - lle - jo,   y   be - sar [té].

Salinas gives other contradictory information by saying that "the discant of *las vacas* usually is interpreted according to the molossus (three long syllables per metric foot) or the ionic" (long-long-short-short).[97] In modern

94 Ward, "Vihuela de mano," 205-206.

95 Francisco de Salinas, *De música Libri septem* (1577). Modern Spanish ed., *Siete libros sobre la música / Francisco Salinas; primera versión castellana por Ismael Fernández de la Cuesta* (Madrid: Alpuerto, 1983), 609.

96 I am grateful to John Griffiths for providing much information and assistance in the development of this text.

97 *Hay que recordar, no obstante, que el discanto* de las vacas *no suele interpretarse según el compás del trocaico, sino del moloso o del jónico…* Salinas, 610.

musical terms, this is triple meter (3/4, with one metric foot equivalent to one musical measure).

Guár - da - me las va - cas, Ca - ri - lle - jo, y be - sar [té].

Salinas also provides an incipit that he identifies as the rhythm of the Italian *Stantia romanescha*, in which the first metrical foot is molossus and the second is ditrochee (long-short-long-short). He cautions the reader to "not believe in the necessity to always form the [phrase] with three trochees (metrical feet consisting of a stressed syllable followed by an unstressed syllable)."[98] In other words, it is possible to have mixed meters.

In the setting by Narváez, there are some measures that are in clearly identifiable rhythmic groupings of either duple or triple meter, and the ease with which Narváez is able to transition from one to the other is apparent. Other measures, such as one and two, are ambiguous, and their interpretation will remain a subjective choice for modern editors and performers. I have chosen 6/8 for measure one because it places the chord-tone G on a strong beat, and 3/4 for measure two because it gives the added interest of a hemiola. If a vocal part is added, there is no reason why variations in accent patterns could not occur spontaneously, becoming mixed and matched between the singer and the instrumentalist. For example, in the instrumental part, the bass in measure three is clearly in 6/8, but the placement of the sixteenth notes in the treble suggests either 3/4 or a syncopation in 6/8. This clever rhythmic alteration by Narváez accommodates the accentuation of *sar* in *besarte* while also preserving the correct metrical structure of the verse (with a single syllable at the end). The singer could (a) choose to adopt this rhythm or (b) simply maintain a trochaic or ionic meter against the syncopated vihuela part.

a Guár - da-me   las   va - cas,   Ca - ri - lle-jo,   y   be-sar   té.   Si

b Guár - da-me   las   va - cas, Ca - ri - lle - jo,   y   be - sar   té.____   Si

8.5. (Otras tres diferencias sobre) Guárdame las vacas. Narváez wrote a second set of three variations that use the same skeletal discant melody as the first four, but he changes the harmonic-bass pattern to another popular form known as the *passamezzo antico*. He describes these variations as *hecho por otra parte* (made on another part), which probably means that the final of the mode is found on another part of the fingerboard. In modern terms, this means that the piece is transposed to a different key [see 5.2]. The change of key suggests that the two sets were conceived independently of one another.[99]

---

98 *He pensado que debía avisar al lector sobre este punto para que no se crea en la necesidad de formar siempre el metro itifálico con tres troqueos.* Ibid., 609.

99 Some modern editors have transposed the first variation of the second set into a-minor and added it to the first set. For an informative article on this, see Nelson Amos, "Luis Narváez, *Guárdame las vacas,* and the *'otra parte'*," *Soundboard*, Summer 2000, 21-25.

The harmonic structure of the *passamezzo antico* is almost identical to the *romanesca*. The main difference is that it begins on the i-chord instead of on III. Also, unlike the *romanesca*, it is not associated with any particular discant melody and therefore is more often found with different melodies—perhaps the most famous today being *Greensleeves*. The most significant differences between the two forms likely had more to do with their overall character than their harmonic progressions. For example, in Galilei's *Primo libro della prattica del contrapunto* (1588-91), the "excited sound of the *romanesca* is compared with the "quiet" one of the *passamezzo*."[100] In this regard, the *passamezzo* is often equated to the *pavana* [see 5.6.5], with which it must have shared a similar or identical dance step. The name, in fact, derives from *pass'e mezzo*, meaning "step and a half."

8.6. Baja de contrapunto (*Baxa de contrapunto*) is a setting of an unknown *baja danza* (Fr. *basse danse*). The dance characteristics are not fully known but are believed to be associated with low movements such as bending or bowing.[101] The music is in triple meter.

8.7. Ya se sienta el Rey Ramiro (*Ya se asienta...*) is a popular *romance* for which Narváez provided three *diferencias* that serve equally well as vocal accompaniment or as an instrumental solo. Before the music, he states that it is in the sixth mode (Hypolydian) and that the first fret on the third course is F (*fe fa ut*), and the third fret of the second string is C (*ce sol fa ut*). From this it can be determined that the "imagined" tuning of his vihuela is D [see 5.2]. The text of the first verse is provided with the tablature. Additional verses, from literary sources, are provided with the transcription.[102] My translation is shown below:

> Now King Ramiro sits down; now he sits for his meal.
> Three of his commanders came and stood before him.
> —"May God keep you, Sir." —"Commanders, welcome.
> And what news do you bring me from Campo de Palomares?"
> —"Good news we bring you, Sir, since we come here.
> We rode for seven days, and never ate bread,
> nor the horses barley, which weighed on us more,
> nor entered into town, nor spoke with anyone
> but for seven hunters who were going out to hunt.
> We did not wish to, but were forced to fight.
> We killed four of them; the other three we bring here.
> And if you don't believe it, good king, they themselves will tell you."

8.8. Conde Claros was another popular *romance* that tells the story of Count Claros who is condemned to death for seducing the king's daughter, Princess Claraniña. The text was published in the *Silva de Romances* [see 5.6.6.1]; however, it probably dates from the previous century or before. The first line of the text (not provided by Narváez) was also taken by Cervantes to open the ninth chapter of *Don Quixote*, perhaps to evoke a humorous comparison to his own love story:

---

100 Giuseppe Gerbino, "Romanesca," *New Grove*, vol. 21, 577.

101 See Kathi Meyer-Baer, "Some Remarks on the Problems of the Basse-Dance," (*Tijdschrift der Vereeniging voor Noord-Nederlands Muziekgeschiedenis*, D. 17de, 4de Stuk, 1955), 251-277, in *JSTOR*, http://links.jstor.org/sici?sici=0921-3260(1955)17%3A4%3C251%3ASROTPO%3E2.0.CO%3B2-F (accessed 10 June 2007).

102 For additional verses and translations, see Thomas Binkley and Margit Frenk, *Spanish Romances of the Sixteenth Century* (Bloomington: Indiana University Press, 1995), 117.

Media noche era por filo; los gallos querian cantar,

Conde Claros con amores, no podía reposar.

Grandes suspiros va dando, que amor le hace penar,

que el amor de Claraniña, no le deja sosegar.

It was about midnight; the roosters wanted to sing.

Count Claros, because of love, is not able to rest.

He heaves great sighs, for love causes him great distress,

and the love of Claraniña will not let him have peace.[103]

In the sixteenth century, one simple formulaic melody and rhythm—consisting of a single phrase—became associated with this *romance*. This served as a basis for singers and instrumentalists to create their own variations. Salinas provides this incipit:[104]

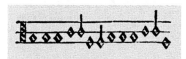

A transcription in modern notation at guitar pitch and with a meter signature is shown below. The exact placement of the vocal text (also provided separately by Salinas) is subject to personal interpretation:

From a modern perspective, the most notable feature of *Conde Claros* is its rhythmic alternation between triple and compound-duple meter. Four known vihuelists wrote *diferencias* on this tune, with the twenty-two by Narváez forming the largest set. All use the harmonic-ground formula: I – IV – V – I.

Insight into how the vihuela and guitar differed from one another in the mind of a sixteenth-century musician is revealed in the fifteenth variation. Here Narváez writes *contrahaciendo la guitarra* (imitating the guitar). He uses only the four inner courses of the vihuela—the interval pattern of the four-course guitar [see 3.2].

---

103 For more verses and translations, see Binkley and Frenk, *Spanish Romances*, 120-130.

104 Salinas, 597.

Fantasía 14

Luis de Narváez

Canción

de Nicolas Gombert

Luis de Narváez

Mille Regretz

Canción del Emperador

Luis de Narváez

66

67

Cuatro diferencias sobre

Guárdame las vacas

Luis de Narváez

68

Otras Tres diferencias sobre

Guárdame las vacas

Luis de Narváez

70

Baja de contrapunto

Luis de Narváez

72

Ya se sienta el rey Ramiro

Romance

Luis de Narváez

74

los tres————————— de sus a-
-da-li-des, se le pa———ra———ron
de———lan————————te, se
le pa———ra———ron———de-lan-te.———

– "Mantenga a vos Dios, señor," – "Adalides, bien vengades. Y ¿qué nuevas me traedes de Campo de Palomares?"
– "Buenas las traes, señor, pues que venimos acá. Siete días anduvimos, que nunca comimos pan,
ni los caballos cebada, de lo que nos pesa más, ni entramos en poblado, ni vimos con quién hablar,
sino siete cazadores, que andaban a cazar. Que nos pesó, nos plugo, hubimos de pelear;
los cuatro de ellos matamos, los tres traemos acá, Y si no lo creéis, buen rey, ellos mismos lo dirán."

Veintidós diferencias sobre

Conde Claros

Luis de Narváez

77

78

–9–

Alonso Mudarra

Tres libros de música was published in Seville in 1546 as a single volume of seventy-seven compositions. Book one, which appears to serve a didactic purpose, begins with ten fantasias—some of which are marked *para desenbolver las manos* (to develop the hands) and others that are marked *fácil* (easy). Two literal intabulations of movements from a mass by Josquin appear next, followed by two variation sets and three dances referred to as *obras menudas* (slight works). Most significantly, it also includes six pieces for the four-course guitar—the first guitar pieces ever published.[105] For the second book, Mudarra organized sets of pieces according to each of the eight modes. These function like suites, although Mudarra did not name them as such. Each begins with a tiento, which fulfills the purpose of a prelude, and is followed by one or more fantasias and intabulations of existing polyphonic vocal works. Book three contains twenty-seven pieces for voice and vihuela, including settings of both secular and Biblical texts. According to James Tyler, Mudarra's secular songs "appear to have been idiomatically conceived for voice and a unique, free-composed vihuela accompaniment. This was most unusual for the time; generally, lute and vihuela songs were merely intabulations of pre-existing part songs. As a composer of secular songs, Mudarra is only equaled, at the end of the century, by John Dowland."[106]

Little is known about Mudarra's life. In the book's dedication to the royal councilor Luis Zapata, Mudarra (ca. 1510-1580) mentions that he had been educated in the household of the third and fourth dukes of the *Infantado* in Guadalajara. When the fourth duke traveled with Charles V to Italy in 1529, it is possible that Mudarra (then about 19 years old), went with him. He entered the priesthood soon afterwards, becoming a canon in the Cathedral of Seville in 1546, and later serving as *mayordomo* (chief of staff) from 1568 until his death in 1580. The provisions of his will indicate that his possessions were to be sold by auction and the proceeds distributed to the poor.[107]

9.1. Fantasía 1 is described by Mudarra as *Fantasia de passos largos para desenbolver las manos* (Fantasia in long passages to develop the hands). It is in two voices of imitative counterpoint that alternate with passages of diminutions called *pasos* or *glosas* [see 5.7.3]. In these first few fantasias, Mudarra specifies the passages to be played *dedillo* or *dos dedos* [see 5.5]. These indications are not reflected in the transcription.

9.2. Pleni sunt de la *Missa Faysan regretz* de Josquin. The Latin *Pleni sunt* refers to the verse *Pleni sunt coeli et terra gloria tua* (Heaven and earth are full of Thy glory) from the Sanctus in the Ordinary of the Mass. A literal transcription of the original, it preserves Josquin's imitative counterpoint derived from the opening motive. There are some changes to accommodate the idiomatic limitations of the vihuela, such as the repetition of long notes that cannot be sustained. A dramatic departure from the original, for reasons unexplained, takes place in one

---

105 See Eric Waters, *Guitar Music from "Tres Libros de Música"* (Pacific, MO: Mel Bay, 2004). All six of Mudarra's guitar pieces are transcribed and thoughtfully edited for modern guitar by Waters, who also provides a new engraving of the tablature and a CD recording.

106 James Tyler, introduction to *Alonso Mudarra: Tres Libros* (Editions Chanterelle: Monaco, 1980), 3.

107 John Griffiths, "Mudarra, Alonso," *New Grove*, vol. 17, 357.

passage (measures 25-30 of my transcription).[108] The dissonances in the final cadence are of special importance to musicologists. We cannot be certain whether these added accidentals originate with Mudarra or whether they reflect regional *música ficta* practices.

9.3. Conde Claros. The story of Count Claros of Montalbán was one of the most popular *romance* themes of sixteenth–century Spain that was used for instrumental variations [see 5.6.6.1 and 8.8].

9.4. Pavana de Alexandre. The bass line to this *pavana* is the Italian *passamezzo antico* ground, but harmonized in the major mode. In the transcription, a modern metrical measure equals three original *compases*. This piece should be played together with the following *Gallarda*. The pairing of these two dances was common in Italy and England, but not in Spain. Mudarra's is the only example in the known vihuela repertoire.

9.5. Gallarda (Galliard). This popular dance piece has been transcribed many times using triple meter (3/4 or 3/2), with one-and-a-half binary *compases* assimilated into a modern measure [see 14.4]. However, triple meter does not accommodate the proper accentuation of the dance, which is characterized by a five-step pattern and a vigorous leap on step five.[109] I believe that a better solution is to combine 6/8 and 3/4 meter, with three *compases* per measure. In this way, the hemiola patterns in measures 15 and 33 also become clear.

9.6. Fantasía 10 is one of the best-known and most celebrated pieces of the entire vihuela repertoire. The text that precedes the music reads: *Fantasia que contrahaze la harpa en la manera de Ludovico. es difficil hasta ser entendida.* (Fantasia that imitates the harp in the manner of Ludovico. It is difficult until understood). This is both a parody and a "disguised set of folia variations that uses cross rhythms and bold chromaticism to imitate the legendary harpist of Ferdinand III of Aragon."[110] Especially noteworthy are the "extended cadential turns played on adjacent strings that allow the pungent melodic minor-second dissonances and cross relations to ring through as they would on the open strings of the harp."[111] At one point in the score (measure 59 in the transcription) Mudarra felt it necessary to explain: "From here until the end there are some dissonances (*falsas*), [that when] played well won't seem bad."

Mudarra's tablature includes a unique symbol, a circumflex (∧) to mark stopped notes that should be sustained longer than the given temporal value; that is, they should be allowed to overlap other notes that follow. In the transcription, I place open-ended slur markings beside these notes when they are inner voices that do not continue, and beside open-string notes that I believe should be interpreted in the same way. This method of notation avoids the excessive use of ties and rests that otherwise would be required. I chose 4:1 tactus reduction with metrical measures comprised of more than one original *compás*. This also suggests using multimetric notation, which I believe is justified in this piece because of its fast tempo and strong rhythmic structures [see 4.6].

---

108 To compare with Josquin's original, see A. Smijers, ed., *Werken Van Josquin De Prez*, vol. 23 (Amsterdam: G. Alsbach & Co., 1951), 47-48.

109 Lawrence H. Moe, "Galliard," *Harvard Dictionary of Music*, 2ⁿᵈ edition, ed. Willi Apel (Cambridge: Harvard University Press, 1975), 340.

110 Griffiths, "Mudarra, Alonso," *New Grove*, 357. Also see John Griffiths, "Mudarra's Harp Fantasia: History and Analysis," *Australian Guitar Journal* 1 (1989): 19-25.

111 Smith, *A History of the Lute*, 235.

My suggested fingerings reflect original fret and string positions of the tablature. An alternative approach, applied frequently to this piece by modern-day guitarists, is to play stepwise notes of scales across different strings so that their sonorities overlap. This technique and musical effect is stylistically associated with music for the Baroque guitar, but not the Renaissance vihuela. It was first described by Gaspar Sanz as *campanelas* (little bells) in his guitar treatise of 1674—more than a century after Mudarra's publication.

9.7. (Piezas del) Tercero Tono. In his second *libro*, as noted above, Mudarra organized sets of pieces according to mode. Each begins with a tiento followed by a fantasia, and then followed by either an intabulation of a polyphonic vocal work or another fantasia, or both. The present set, in the Phrygian mode, consists of three pieces, the third of which is an intabulation with the inscription: *Glosa sobre un Kyrie postrero de una misa de Josquin que va sobre Pange Lingua* (Glosa on a posterior Kyrie from a Mass by Josquin on Pange Lingua). Josquin's *Missa Pange lingua*, which is considered one of the polyphonic masterpieces of the Renaissance, is based on a plainchant setting of the hymn "Sing, my tongue" by St. Thomas Aquinas (1225-1274). Mudarra identifies passages of literal transcription by writing Josquin's name in the tablature, while marking his own freely composed sections with the term *glosa*.

9.8. Triste estaba el rey David (*Triste estava…*) is a *romance* from the Biblical story (2 Samuel 3:3) of David, King of the Jews, and his estranged son, Absalom, who had tried to overthrow him. David's army was able to quell the revolution and capture Absalom, who was then killed against the king's orders. Mudarra shortened and adapted the text, which translates:

> Sad was King David, sad and with great grief,
>
> when they brought him news of the death of Absalom.
>
> He spoke sad words, which came from the heart:
>
> "They were the cause of your death and my grief.
>
> I did not want to see you dead, but alive in my prison.
>
> For, though you were disobedient, I would have forgiven you,
>
> my son."

The voice part appears on a separate staff in mensural notation above the vihuela tablature. Mudarra used this combination to notate his original vocal works in which there is an independent vihuela accompaniment. For his intabulations of existing vocal polyphony, he simply added *puntillos* (small oblique slashes) beside the ciphers of a designated part that could be both sung and played.

9.9. Isabel, perdiste la tu faja (*Ysabel, perdiste la tu faxa*) is a *villancico* with a lighthearted and metaphorical text about love and virginity:

> Isabel, Isabel, you have lost your belt.[112]
> There it goes floating in the water!
> Lovely Isabel![113]

According to Stephen Haynes, the belt is "a conventional emblem of chastity—Isabel has undoubtedly lost something more important than a fashion accessory."[114]

Plate 12
King David playing a harp.
Engraving from Mudarra's *Tres libros de música*

---

112 Literally: "girdle."

113 Stephen Haynes, trans., performance notes for Catherine King and Jacob Heringman, *Alonso Mudarra: Spanish Songs and Vihuela Solos*, Gaudeamus CD GAU 162.

114 Ibid.

Te canam magni Iouis, et deorum ꝑ Horatiꝰ lib.
Nuntium, Curux ꝗ liræ parentem. ꝑ ɪ. Carmiñ.

Plate 13
Mercury playing a lyre
Mercury, the winged messenger of the gods, is said to have made a lyre from the shell of a turtle.
Engraving from Mudarra's *Tres libros de música*.

Fantasía 1

Alonso Mudarra

84

Pleni sunt

de la *Missa Faysan regretz* de Josquin

Alonso Mudarra

Diferencias sobre
Conde Claros

Alonso Mudarra

89

Pavana de Alexandre

Alonso Mudarra

Gallarda

Alonso Mudarra

91

Fantasía 10

que contrahace la harpa en la manera de Ludovico

Alonso Mudarra

Desde aquí hasta acerca del final hay algunas falsas, tañiéndose bien no parecen mal.

Tercer Tono

Alonso Mudarra

Tiento

Fantasía

95

97

Glosa sobre un Kyrie de Josquin

Sobre Pange Lingua

Triste estaba el rey David

Romance

Alonso Mudarra

Tris - te es - ta - ba el rey Da - vid,_____
Cuan - do le vi - nie - ron nue - - - -

vas_____
tris - te y con gran pa -
de la muer - te de Ab - sa -

- - - síon,_____ cuan - - - do le vi -
- - - lón._____ Pa - - - la - bras tris -

-nie - - ron nue - - - - - vas_____
-tes de - cí - - - - - a,

"Ellos mismos fueron causa
de tu muerte y mi pasión,
No te quisiera ver muerto
sino vivo en mi prisión.

No te quisiera ver muerto
sino vivo en mi prisión,
que aunque me eras desobediente,
yo te otorgara perdón,
fili mi."

Isabel, perdiste la tu faja

Villancico

Alonso de Mudarra

I - sa - bel,   I - sa - bel,   per - dis -

-te la_____ tu fa - - ja ¡É - la por do va, na-

-dan-do por el a - - gua, por_____ el a - - gua!

¡É - la, por do va, na - dan-do por el

103

–10–

Enríquez de Valderrábano

In 1547, one year after Mudarra's publication, Valderrábano released his *Libro de música de vihuela, intitulado Silva de sirenas* (Sylvan wood of Sirens). According to Greek and Roman mythology, the sirens were sea nymphs––part woman and part bird—whose seductive songs would lure mariners to their deaths on rocky shores. Valderrábano's title evokes one of Homer's stories about Odysseus (*Odyssey* XII, 39*)*, who commanded his sailors to put wax in their ears so that they could navigate safely and to tie him to the ship's mast so that he could hear the sirens' seductive call.

Griffiths:

> It was probably the dedication of Enríquez de Valderrábano's *Silva de sirenas* to Francisco de Zúñiga and the reference to him as a resident of Peñaranda de Duero that lead Juan Bermudo to assume him to have been a musician in the service of the Count of Miranda, but contemporary research has failed to uncover any trace of his life. All that remains is his anthology of 171 solo pieces and songs, both original works and arrangements of music by other lutenists and vocal composers. The style of his solo music is highly individual and somewhat enigmatic, and his fantasias proceed as long discourses that often borrow extensively from the music of other composers, but with relatively little of the polyphonic imitation that is the structural nucleus of the music of other instrumental composers.[115]

Valderrábano's publication was known abroad, and selections from it have been found in anthologies collected in other countries.[116] It is in seven *libros*, generally graded by level of difficulty. The first has two *fugas* and imitative compositions in three parts, with one in red ink to designate it as an optional vocal part, although no text is provided. Books two and three contain music for voice and vihuela, including intabulations of motets and secular music by composers such as Arcadelt, Gombert, Jacquet, Josquin, Morales, Willaert, and others. Book four has the only known intabulations for two vihuelas, with one part printed upside down so that it can be read from the other side of a table. Book five has thirty-three fantasias, nineteen of which are parodies of vocal works [see 5.6.1]. Book six contains solo works, including ones that Valderrábano calls *sonetos*, but which are probably better described as *villancicos* [see 10.3]. Book seven is a group of *pavanas*.

10.1. Fantasía 1. Valderrábano identifies this fantasia by mode (*cuatro tono*) and by level of difficulty (*Primero grado*). The nominal tuning is E, like that of the modern guitar. The transposed Hypophrygian mode is B, C, D, E, F, G, A, B.

10.2. Fantasía 19. The text preceding this work reads: *Fantasia remedada al chirie postrero de la misa de losquin, De beata virgine. Primero tono, Segundo grado* (Parody fantasia on the posterior kyrie of Josquin's mass of

---

115 Griffiths, "The Two Renaissances," 6.

116 For example, Phalèse printed fourteen works by Valderrábano in his *Hortus Musarum* (1552-53).

the blessed virgin. First mode, second level). Griffiths states: "The fantasia borrows extensively from the model with sixty-six of its 129 *compases* being quotations from the mass section. In addition, it is a work which shows Valderrábano to have parodied elements of the design of the model."[117]

10.3. Agnus Dei, de Cristóbal de Morales is a literal intabulation of the second "Agnus Dei" setting from *Missa Vulnerasti cor meum* by Morales. Valderrábano writes that it is level one and in three parts. "The stylistic influence of Josquin is clearly evident. What is equally notable is the rapidity with which Valderrábano incorporated the work into *Silva de sirenas* only three years after the first edition appeared, an indication of the desire of vihuelists to be up-to-date with the latest and most advanced works of master polyphonists."[118]

10.4. Soneto and **Soneto lombardo a manera de danza.** Valderrábano wrote twenty-seven compositions that he called *sonetos*, twenty-two of which are small instrumental pieces. The other five are accompanied vocal works (three of which are also identified as *villancicos* in the table of contents). Valderrábano's use of the term *soneto* is imprecise. His works by this name appear to have no connection to literary sonnets or musical *sonetos* of other vihuelists [see 5.6.6.3]. Pujol has speculated that he may have used it as a diminutive of *son*, to mean, "little tune."[119] The two that I have selected are an unrelated pair, but work well together. The first is identified only as *Soneto, Primero grado,* and has an accompanying text that tells us it is in the proportion of three *minimas* to the *compás*. The second, *Soneto lombardo a manera de dança, Primero grado*, is a version of an Italian *pavana* that also appears in German and French collections for the lute and organ. Lutenist Hans Newsidler called the tune *Welschertanz* (Italian dance).

10.5. Siete diferencias fáciles sobre Guárdame las vacas. These attractive variations are very different from those of Narváez [see 8.4], although they are based on the same melodic-harmonic formula of the *romanesca*. I chose the meter of 3/2 instead of 3/4 to avoid having thirty-second notes in variation seven. Players should determine their tempo with this last variation in mind.

---

117 Griffiths, "The Vihuela Fantasia," 266. On pages 264-273, Griffiths analyzes the parody techniques used in this fantasia. Josquin's original composition is reprinted in: Josquin de Pres, *Werken*, 30, ed. A. Smijers (Amsterdam: Vereniging voor Nederlandse Muziekgeschiedenis, 1952), 127-128.

118 Griffiths, "How to Play the Vihuela According to Juan Bermudo," 10.

119 Navarrete, "The Problem of the *Soneto*," 780.

LIBRO DE MVSICA

DE VIHVELA, INTITVLADO SILVADE

sirenas, En el qual se hallara toda diuersidad de musica, Compuesto por Enrriqʒ
de Valderrauano. Dirigido al Illustrisimo señor don Francisco de Çuñiga Cõ
de de Miranda. Señor de las casas de Auellaneda y Baçan.&c,

CON PRIVILEGIO IMPERIAL,

Estan tassados en dos ducados

Plate 14

The cover of Valderrábano's *Silva de sirenas*

Fantasía 1

Enríquez de Valderrábano

Fantasía 19

Enríquez de Valderrábano

Soneto

Enríquez de Valderrábano

113

Soneto lombardo a manera de danza

Enríquez de Valderrábano

Agnus dei, de Morales

de la *Missa Vulnerasti cor meum*

Enríquez de Valderrábano

Siete diferencias faciles, sobre

Guárdame las vacas

Enríquez de Valderrábano

119

120

Diego Pisador

Pisador (ca. 1509/10–after 1577), a citizen of Salamanca, took minor religious orders in 1526 without becoming a priest, but obtained the post of *mayordomo* of the city in 1532. His *Libro de música de vihuela* was self-published at his expense in 1552. It is divided into seven parts totaling ninety-five works—twenty-six fantasias, twenty-two intabulations of polyphonic vocal works (including transcriptions of eight complete masses of Josquin), forty-six songs, and one dance.

Pisador was not a professional musician, and deficiencies become apparent in his polyphonic works. Ward speculates that Bermudo may have had Pisador in mind when he wrote:

> I say truly that I have copied the counterpoint of a player of the vihuela (and not a player of ill fame), written in ciphers, into notes: which has been not a little laughed at among singers [*cantores*]. Since it is not my business to malign, I omit the name of the player.[120]

Griffiths gives his assessment:

> Even when one resolves the typographical errors that abound in his tablature, it is evident that his compositional ability was limited. In his fantasias, Pisador was neither able to control the density of musical texture nor direct the flow of his harmony with great skill. There is a frustrating and un-reconciled tension between his ability to conceive satisfying musical forms and his lack of ability to bring his intentions to fruition. On the other hand, his *diferencias* and songs, which are of modest pretensions are more satisfying works in performance.[121]

I had wanted to provide representative examples of original fantasias by each of the vihuelists, but those of Pisador fall too short of the standard set by the others to warrant inclusion in a selective anthology.[122] As previously mentioned, Pisador is at his best with intabulations of other composers, and his vocal works are among the most successful pieces in his book. Some are given as vihuela solos while others provide a text with the voice part shown either on a separate staff in mensural notation or in red ink as part of the vihuela tablature. All may be played as solos since the voice line is integrated into the vihuela arrangement.

11.1. Pavana. The title in Pisador's book is *Pavana muy llana para tañer* (Pavana, very plain [unadorned] to play). It is in three voices and follows an Italian melody that became known internationally as *La Cara Cosa* and *La Gamba*. This melody is also built on a chord progression (V-i-VII-III-VII-i-V-i) that later—with the addition of an opening tonic-chord (i)—became known as the *folía*, which was immensely popular during the next century as a basis for variations. Pisador uses hemiola simply but effectively in measures 18-19 and 22-23.

---

120 Bermudo, *Declaración*, 100', trans. Ward, "The Vihuela de mano," 387.

121 Griffiths, "The Two Renaissances," 7.

122 The complete works of Pisador are now available in guitar transcriptions, with facsimiles and critical commentary in Spanish by Francisco Roa and Felipe Gértrudix (see footnote 13).

11.2. Decirle al caballero (*Dezilde al cavallero*)[123] is a *villancico* for which Pisador does not provide a text or an identified voice part. The text is found as the *cantus firmus* in a polyphonic setting by the Flemish composer Nicolas Gombert in the *Cancionero de Upsala* [see 5.6.6.1 and 5.6.6.2]. Translated into English, it reads:

> Tell the knight not to grieve, for I give him my word that I will not leave him.
> Tell the handsome knight not to grieve in hiding,
> for I give him my word that I will not leave him.

11.3. Si la noche hace oscura (*Si la noche haze escura*) was a popular *villancico* text throughout the sixteenth century, as evidenced by the large number of variants that survive.[124] A translation of Pisador's version is shown below:

> If the night is dark and the way so short,
> how is it that you do not come, friend?
> If midnight is passed and the one who torments me does not come,
> my misfortune stops him because I am so unlucky.
> I see myself forsaken; I harbor great passion.
> How is it that you do not come, friend?

The setting is in three voices, with the vocal part doubled by the vihuela and written in red ink as part of the tablature. Pisador tells us that the note C (ce sol fa ut) is found on the third course in the third fret. From this, we know that the piece is in mode IV (Hypophrygian). On the modern guitar this becomes B, C, D, E, F, G, A, B.

11.4. ¿Y con qué la lavaré?. Pisador's setting of this *villancico* is in imitative polyphony and is similar to a version by Juan Vásquez found in the *Cancionero de Upsala*. It is in three voices, with the vocal part identified in red ink. Other voice and vihuela arrangements of this song were made by Narváez, Valderrábano, and Fuenllana [see 12.4]. Perhaps of Mediterranean origin, it also survives in French sources as *Sur le mont de Sion* and as *Sur le pont d'Avignon*. Pisador's version of the text is translated:

> And with what should I wash, the flower of, my face?
> And with what should I wash it, since I live with such suffering?
> Young girls should wash themselves with lemon water.
> I wash myself with anxieties and sorrows.

---

123 It has been assumed that the inversion of the letters d and l in the original was a typographical error. However, Griffiths informs me that he has found the same spelling ("dezilde") in other early texts such as Milán's 1535 *Libro de motes*.

124 See Margit Frenk, *Corpus de la Antigua Lírica Popular Hispánica* (Madrid: Castalia, 1987), 264-265.

LIBRO DE MVSICA DE
VIHVELA, AGORA NVEVA
mente compuesto por Diego Pisador, ve
zino dela ciudad de Salamanca, dirigido al muy alto y muy poderoso
señor don Philippe princi
pe de España nue
stro Señor.

CON PRIVILEGIO.
Esta tassado en   marauedis.
1552

Plate 15

The cover of Pisador's *Libro de música de vihuela*

Pavana

Diego Pisador

Decirle al caballero

Villancico

Diego Pisador

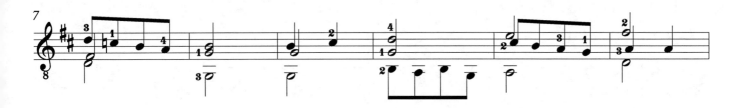

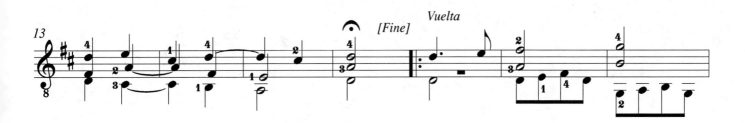

Decirle al caballero que no se queje, que yo le doy mi fe que no le deje.

Decirle al caballero, cuerpo garrido, que no se queje en escondido,

que yo le doy mi fe que no le deje.

Si la noche hace oscura

Villancico

Diego Pisador

Si la no - che ha - ce os cu - ra y tan
Ve - o me de - sam - pa - ra - da gran pa -

cor - to es el ca - mi - no,
sión ten - go con mi - go,

¿có - mo no ve - nís a -

mi - - go?

¿có - mo no vie - nes a - mi - - go? [Fine]

Vuelta

Si la me - dia no - che es pa - sa -
Mi ven - tu - ra lo de - tie - ne por -

da y el que me pe - na no____ vie - ne,____ [D.C. al Fine]
que soy muy des - di - cha - - da.____

¿Y con qué la lavaré?

Villancico de Juan Vásquez

Diego Pisador

qué la la - va - ré.

-var - me yo cui - ta - da

la flor de

con an - sias

la mi ca - - - ra?

y do - lo - - - res.

¿Y con

qué la la - va - ré?

que vi - vo mal___ pe - na - - da.

¿Y con qué la la-va-ré? que vi-vo mal____ pe-na____ da.____

[Fine] Vuelta

Lá_____ van se las mo____

____zas, con a-gua de li-mo____

____nes, con a-gua de li-mo____nes.____

[D.C. al Fine]

129

–12–

Miguel de Fuenllana

The earliest record of Fuenllana dates from 1553 when he was issued a printing license in Valladolid. From this, we know that his birthplace is Navalcarnero (near Madrid). His *Libro de música para vihuela intitulado orphenica lyra* (Orphic lyre) was published in Seville one year later. In the book's dedication, to Prince Philip, Fuenllana informs us that he was blind since infancy.[125] Bermudo referred to him as a "consummate player" and tells of an occasion in which he played on a vihuela *destemplada* (tuned in an unusual manner).[126]

Griffiths states:

> Without any doubt, Miguel de Fuenllana is one of the most outstanding instrumental composers of the sixteenth century and still largely underestimated. He is a composer who deserves to be included among the most outstanding instrumental musicians of the sixteenth century alongside Antonio de Cabezón, Francesco da Milano, William Byrd, John Dowland, or any other acknowledged Renaissance master. In considering the only surviving source of Fuenllana's music, it should be remembered that *Orphénica lyra* (1554) was published when he was probably still in his early twenties, and we can only guess what he might have achieved in the following thirty or forty years of his musical career. At the time of the book's publication, Fuenllana was in Seville, but the following year the theorist Juan Bermudo cites him as being a musician of the Marquesa of Tarifa. Although not independently confirmed, the probability of this is supported by his subsequent appointment to the royal court in 1560 as a chamber musician to Felipe II's second wife, Isabel de Valois, immediately following the marchioness' departure for Naples where her husband, the Duke of Alcalá, had been appointed viceroy. Fuenllana spent more than thirty years in court service.[127]

Orphénica lyra is divided by genre into six *libros* containing 160 pieces for six-course vihuela, nine for five-course vihuela, and nine for four-course guitar. Approximately two-thirds are intabulations of existing vocal works. The original compositions include fifty-one fantasias, eight tientos, two duos (contrapuntal exercises in two voices), a *glosa* on *Tant que vivray*, and an original motet—*Benedicamus patrem*.[128] Many of Fuenllana's compositions are "strongly architectonic works that conceal a high level of expression within their dense counterpoint. It is very difficult music, and this is undoubtedly a principal factor that continues to make it the least heard vihuela music today."[129]

---

125 Fol. 11ᵛ. *Y puesto que a la bondad Divina, por oculto juyzio suyo, le plugo desde mi infancia privarme de la luz corporal.* (And since in Divine goodness, by hidden judgment, it pleased him to deprive me from my infancy of corporeal light...)

126 Bermudo, *Declaración*, fols. 30ʳ and 101ʳ, cited in Ward, "The Vihuela de Mano," 364.

127 Griffiths, "The Two Renaissances," 8.

128 Griffiths, "Fuenllana, Miguel de," *New Grove*, vol. 9. 313. Some books list fifty-two fantasías because they include the *Benedicamus patrem* motet in this category.

129 Griffiths, "The Two Renaissances," 8.

Besides giving us the largest single collection of vihuela music, Fuenllana provides information on the evolution of vihuela technique and performance practice. He recommends alternating the index and middle fingers to pluck the strings instead of the *dedillo* and *dos dedos* techniques of earlier vihuelists [see 5.5.1]. Furthermore, his explanation of how to practice modes on "any part of the vihuela" suggests that he used an instrument tuned in equal temperament.[130]

12.1. Duo. "An abstract work in two voices, this duo that Fuenllana included among the easy pieces at the beginning of *Orphénica lyra* is the only two-voiced fantasia that is preserved in the extant repertory for vihuela. It...is identifiable with the instrumental fantasia genre due to its construction from various imitative sections separated by cadences."[131]

12.2. Fantasía 27. Like most of Fuenllana's polyphonic works, this fantasia is modeled after vocal music. It "is one of those fantasias that can easily be understood as a type of 'instrumental motet' built from independent sections separated by cadences and based on a variety of imitative techniques. The interpretation of this type of work requires the instrumentalist to seek out the identity of each theme and musical paragraph, albeit very abstract given the absence of a sung text."[132] The suggested fingering in measure nine does not allow the bass note to sustain. Other fingerings that make the sustain possible are substantially more difficult. With rubato phrasing, an abrupt detachment of this note can be avoided [see 7.3].

12.3. Tan[t] que vivray is Fuenllana's setting of a widely-known French *chanson* by Claudin de Sermisy (c. 1490-1562). The text, by Clèment Marot, translates: "As long as I live in a flowering age, I shall serve the powerful god Love, in deeds, words, songs and harmony."[133] Fuenllana also provides a *glosa sobre la misma canción* (gloss on the same song), his only embellished version of a vocal work. "Although, in the prologue of *Orphénica lyra* (fol. v), he admonishes the use of excessive embellishment in intabulations, he also clearly acknowledges the existence of the practice that is evident in the music of contemporaries such as Diego Ortiz and Antonio de Cabezón [see 5.7.3]. These composers utilized French chansons as a vehicle for showing their art of embellishment, a practice that in Italy converted the *chanson* into one of the new instrumental forms of the later sixteenth century, the *canzona*."[134]

12.4. ¿Con qué la lavaré? is one of many settings of this popular *villancico* by Juan Vásquez.[135] The text selected by Fuenllana is translated:

> With what should I wash, the flower of, my face?
> With what should I wash it, since I live with such suffering?
> Married women should wash themselves with lemon water.

---

130 Griffiths, "Fuenllana, Miguel de," *New Grove*, 313.

131 Ibid., 13.

132 Griffiths, "How to Play the Vihuela According to Juan Bermudo," 14.

133 Trans. Griffiths, Ibid., 10.

134 Ibid. 11.

135 See 11.4 for another version by Pisador. Other vihuela arrangements are by Narváez and Valderrábano.

I wash myself well with anxieties and sorrows.

With what should I wash it, since I live with so much suffering?[136]

12.5. De Antequera sale el moro is an intabulation of a *romance viejo* setting in four voices by Cristóbal de Morales. The text is unusual in that it expresses the Moorish perspective regarding the fall of Antequera in 1410. Fuenllana provides only the first verse, which is included in the transcription. Additional verses are found in literary sources, a few of which are provided below the music.[137] Performers who wish to include them will need to make adjustments to the rhythmical divisions of the music. My translation is shown below:

> The Moor set out from Antequera; from Antequera he went forth.
>
> He carried letters in his hand, letters containing messages.
>
> A hundred and twenty years, the Moor; two hundred he seemed.
>
> His beard was white, very long, down to his waist.
>
> He encountered the king, who was leaving from the Alhambra
>
> with two hundred on horseback, the best he had.
>
> When he came before the king, he said:
>
> —"May God keep Your Highness; may God save Your Lordship."
>
> —"Welcome, old Moor. For days I have awaited you.
>
> What news do you bring, o Moor, from my village Antequera?"
>
> —"The news, my king, you know is not happy news,
>
> for Prince Don Fernando has surrounded your village.
>
> The Moors that were within are eating cowhides.
>
> If you do not help, o king, your village will be lost."

12.6. Fantasía 40. Fuenllana provides the earliest known source of music for the five-course vihuela [see 2.3]. His works for this instrument include six fantasias, parts of a mass by Morales, and one *villancico*. The interval pattern for this *vihuela de cinco ordenes* is the same as on the modern guitar; that is, the third course is tuned a half step higher than on the normal six-course vihuela.

12.7. Fantasía 46 is one of six fantasias by Fuenllana that were written for four-course guitar. His other guitar works include a three-voice setting of *Crucifixus est* and two works for voice and guitar—a *villancico* and a *romance*.

12.8. Fantasía 51 is not typical of Fuenllana's compositional style. All of his other fantasias are modeled after vocal polyphony and avoid excursions of instrumental embellishment. The present work, however, uses idiomatic *redobles* [see 5.7] as the foundation for its construction. The accompanying caption is translated: "Following is a fantasia of *redobles* composed by the author. It is of much benefit to develop the hands, and to have some information about gallant *redobles* and good diminution."[138]

---

136 Variations of the text in sixteenth-century sources may be found in Eduardo Sohns, "Seis versions del villancico *Con qué la lavaré* en los cancioneros españoles del siglo XVI." *Revista de Musicología*, vol. 10, no. 1, 1987: 173-220.

137 *Pliegos poéticos góticos de la Biblioteca Nacional*, vol. III (Madrid, 1958), 98, reprinted and trans. Binkley and Frenk, *Spanish Romances*, 113-114.

138 *Siguese una fantasia de redobles compuesta por el author, es de mucho provecho para desembolver las manos, y para tener alguna noticia de redobles galanos y de Buena diminucion.*

Plate 16

The cover of Fuenllana's *Orphénica lyra*

Duo

Miguel de Fuenllana

Fantasía 27

Miguel de Fuenllana

Tant que vivray

Canción de Claudin de Sermisy

Miguel de Fuenllana

Glosa

139

¿Con qué la lavaré?

Villancico a cuatro de Juan Vásquez

Miguel de Fuenllana

140

De Antequera sale el moro

Romance de Cristóbal de Morales

Miguel de Fuenllana

men - - sa - - - - je rí - - a.

Ciento y veinte años el moro, de doscientos parecía.
La barba llevaba blanca, muy larga, hasta la cinta.

Encontrado há con el rey, que del Alhambra salía,
con docientos de a caballo, los mejores que tenía.

Ante el rey cuando se halla tales palabras decía:
– "Mantenga Dios a su Alteza, salve Dios tu Señoría."

– "Bien vengas, el moro viejo; días ha que te atendía.
¿Qué nuevas me traes, el moro, de Antequera esa mi villa?"

– "Las nuevas que, rey, sabrás no son nuevas de alegría,
que ese Infante Don Fernando cercada tiene tu villa.

Los moros que estaban dentro, cueros de vaca comían.
Si no socorres, el rey, tu villa se perdería."

Fantasía 40

Miguel de Fuenllana

145

Fantasía 46

Miguel de Fuenllana

147

Fantasía 51

de redobles

Miguel de Fuenllana

Esteban Daza

Almost nothing was known about Esteban Daza (Estevan Daça) until research by John Griffiths led to a published account in 1995.[139] Thanks to this study, we now know that Daza was born into a large and once prestigious family in Valladolid, probably in late 1537.[140] Griffiths believes Daza was "a recluse who retreated into a hermetic existence."[141] Although he was educated at the University of Valladolid (most likely a student of law) there is no suggestion that he ever practiced a profession. "Nor did he venture far from the family fold: unmarried at fifty, he continued to reside with four of his younger siblings, and at the end of his life was buried in the family chapel at San Benito el Real."[142]

In 1575 Daza was granted a printing license for his *Libro de música en cifras para vihuela, intitulado El parnasso* (The Parnassus). The book appeared in 1576, twenty-two years after Fuenllana's *Orphénica lyra*, and was the last tablature collection published for the vihuela. Named after the mountain home of the classical muses, *El Parnasso* is divided into three *libros*, the first of which contains twenty-two fantasias:

> Fourteen of the fantasias are in four-part voicing, four are in three parts, and four consist largely of passage work (to develop the hands). All are marked with either "F" indicating *facil* (easy) or "D" for *difícil*. Daza's fantasias make use of two styles: the first uses imitative techniques found in sixteenth century motets; the second is based on the idiomatic potential of the vihuela. The first style is exhibited in the first eighteen fantasias in which Daza uses small oblique slashes (*puntillos*) beside the tablature numbers to indicate the tenor or alto voice. The second style is exhibited in the last four fantasias which may be regarded as "instrumental motets" rather than pure improvisatory musical fantasy.[143]

The second book includes intabulations of polyphonic vocal motets by leading Franco-Flemish and Spanish composers, and six by a lesser-known French composer, Simon Boyleau. As in his fantasias, Daza again uses *puntillos* to designate one part (usually the tenor) that may be sung as well as played. He places the text below the staff.

Book three consists of twenty-five Spanish secular songs—*sonetos, villanescas, villancicos*, and a *romance*—and two French *chansons* (*canciones francsas*). They too are notated with *puntillos* to indicate the part that is to be sung, if desired, but work equally well as vihuela solos.

---

139 John Griffiths, "Esteban Daza: A Gentleman Musician in Renaissance Spain," *Early Music*, vol. 23, no. 3, (Aug., 1995): 437-448.

140 Ibid., 439.

141 Ibid.

142 Griffiths, "The Two Renaissances," 5.

143 John Griffiths, *Esteban Daza: The Fantasias for Vihuela, Recent Researches in the Music of the Renaissance*, vol. 54, (A.R. Editions: Madison, Wisconsin, 1982), xi.

Further study is needed to assess Daza's rightful place among the Spanish vihuelists. In 1980 Ward dismissed his work as "a rather bland conclusion to the series of vihuela tablatures."[144] Griffiths contends, however, that Daza was "a man who was eloquent and fluent in his music expression, who was competent and thorough as a composer, and who was probably an advanced instrumental technician."[145]

13.1. Fantasía 12. The original caption is *Fantasia a 3 por el primer tono* (Fantasia in three [voices], in the first mode). Griffiths: "This is one of four easy fantasias in three voices. The close agreement between these works and the rules provided by Tomás de Santa María in his *Arte de tañer fantasia* (Valladolid, 1565) suggests that Daza might have learnt composition from this treatise. They are rigorously polyphonic fantasias that require the performer take care in shaping the themes and making the most of the imitative interplay. The cadential ornaments help to articulate the structure of the work."[146]

13.2. Fantasía 21 and **Fantasía 22** are designated as being *de passos largos para desemvoluer las manos* (of long passages to develop the hands) because they contain extended passages of diminutions. Although marked "D" for *difícil*, they are idiomatically conceived and therefore fall naturally on the fingerboard. A symbol believed to indicate a slow tempo is shown at the beginning of the tablature.

13.3. Nunca más verán mis ojos is Daza's setting of an anonymous *villancico*, the lyrics of which are translated:

> Never again will my eyes see anything that gives them pleasure,
> until they see you return.
> Since my eyes have lost the good they found in you,
> hope has abandoned them.
> Why they were born I do not know.
> Because they are away from you, they will have no pleasure
> until they see you again.

---

144 John Ward, *New Grove*, 1st ed., vol. 5 (1980), 288.

145 Griffiths, *Esteban Daza: The Fantasias*, vii.

146 Griffiths, "How to Play the Vihuela According to Juan Bermudo," 13.

Fantasía 12

Esteban Daza

152

Fantasía 21

Esteban Daza

154

155

Fantasía 22

Esteban Daza

Nunca más verán mis ojos

Villancico

Esteban Daza

ros a — ver, has - ta tor - na - - - - - ros —

— a - ver has - ta tor - na - - ros, has - ta tor -

[Fine]

- na - - ros —— a - - ver ———

Vuelta

Pues que mis o - jos per - di - -
si les fal - ta la e - spe - - -

[D.C. al Fine]

- e - ron —— el bien que de vos se al - can - za.
- ran - za. —— No se pa - ra que na - cie - ron.

159

–14–

Facsimiles

These facsimiles were made from exemplars of the original books that are now preserved at the Biblioteca Nacional in Madrid: Luis Milán (R. 9281 and R. 14752), Luis de Narváez (R. 9741), Alonso Mudarra (R. 14630), Enríquez de Valderrábano (R. 14018), Diego Pisador (R. 14060 and R. 9280), Miguel de Fuenllana (R. 9283), and Esteban Daza (R. 14611 and R. 8870). The images were provided by Carlos González and are used with permission [see 1.5]. In the originals, to avoid unused space on costly paper, it was customary to begin a new piece on the same line as the end of the previous piece. The facsimiles in this anthology have been edited to remove the extraneous music and text of these adjacent pieces.

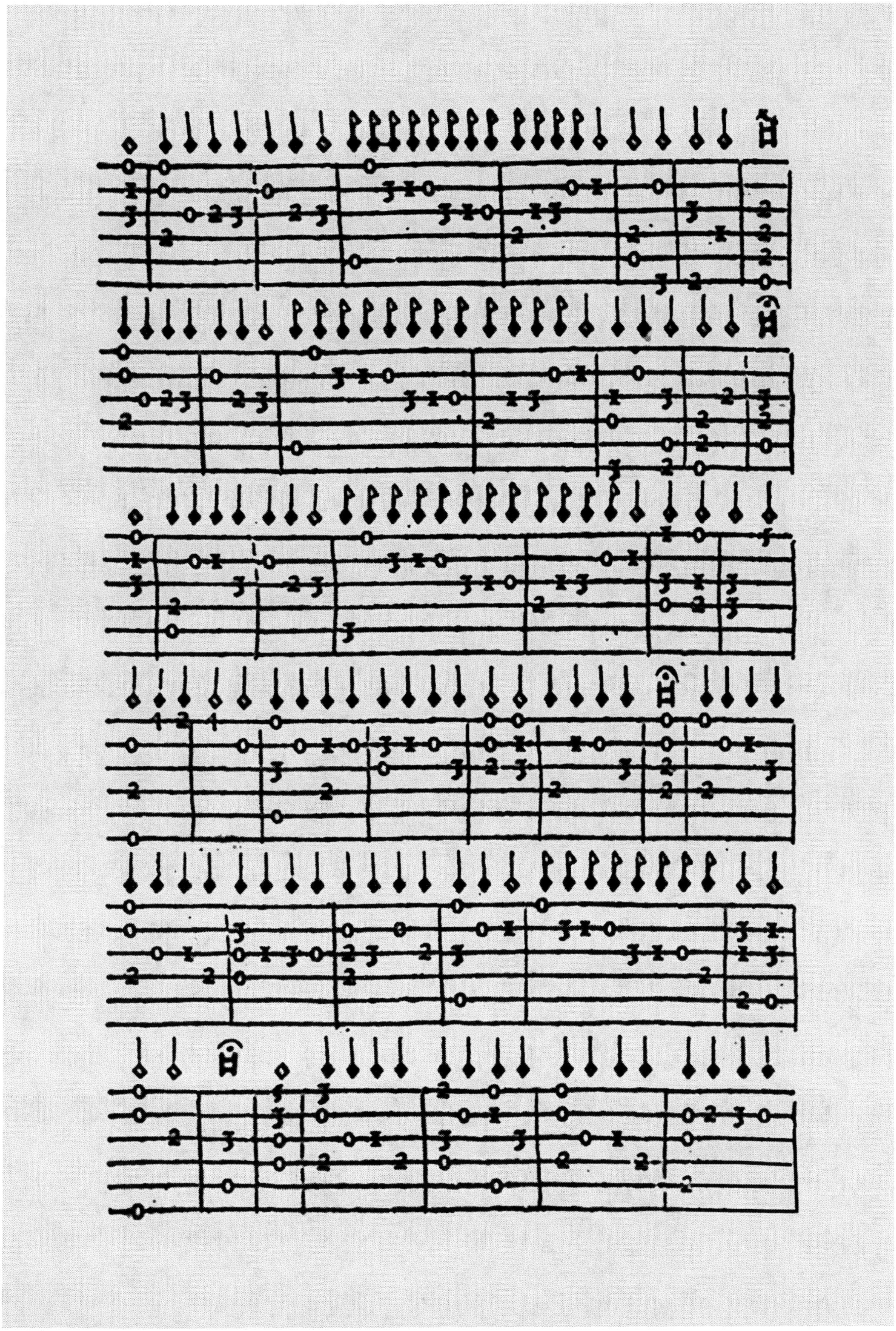

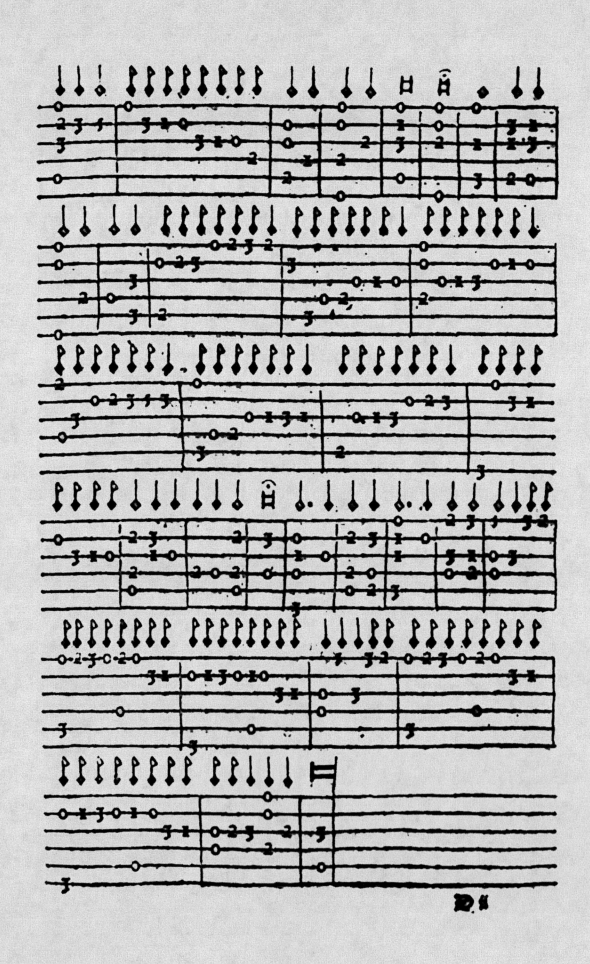

162

14.2   Luis de Narváez: *Mille Regretz*

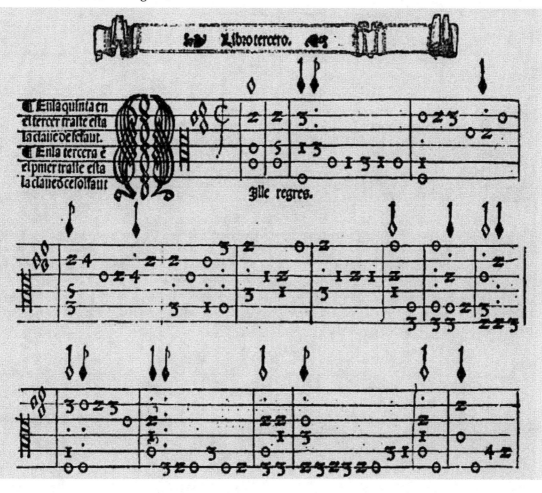

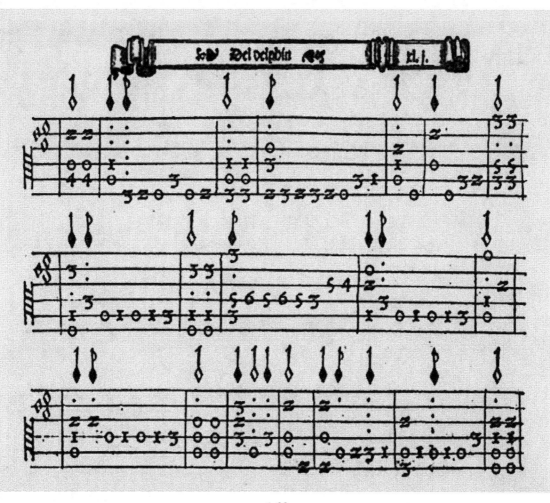

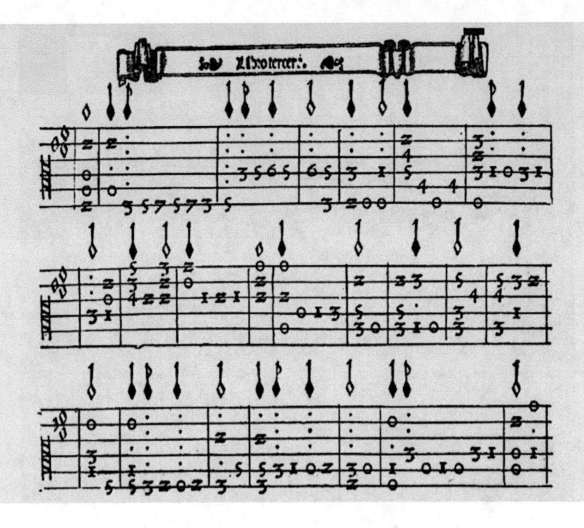

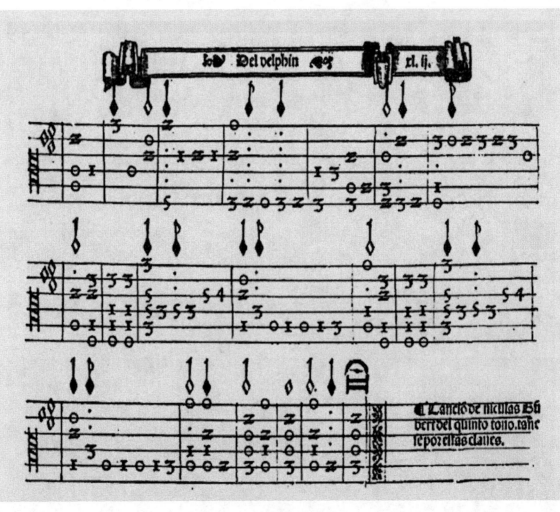

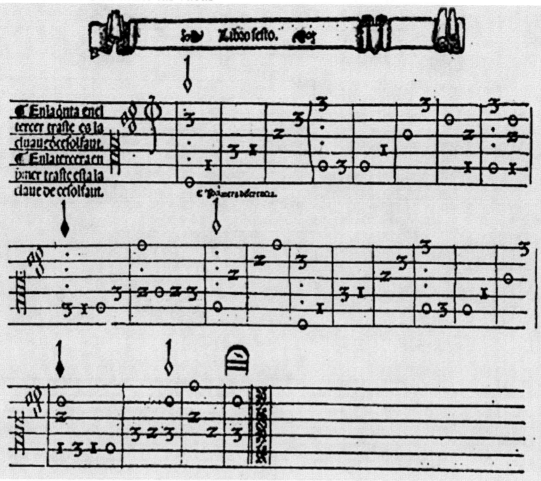

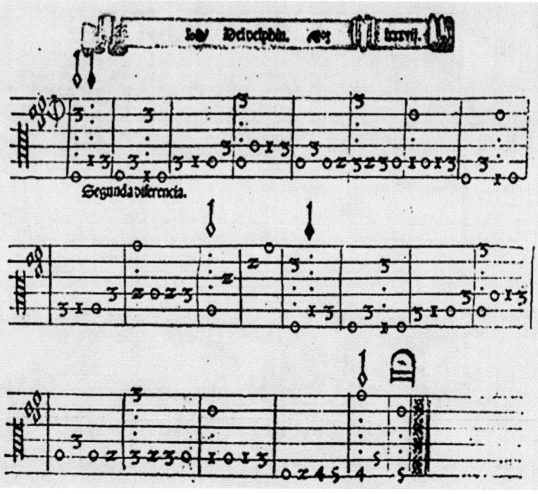

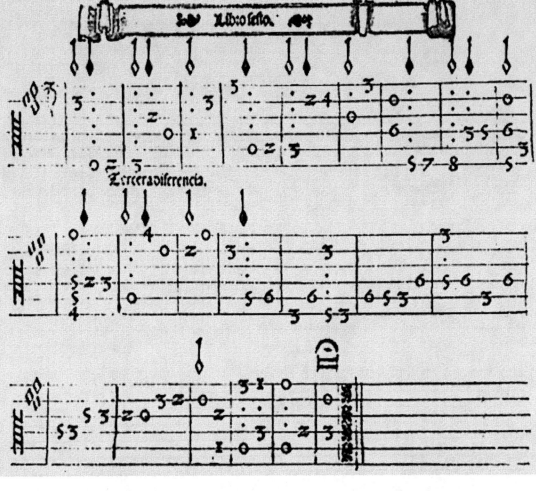

Tercera diferencia.

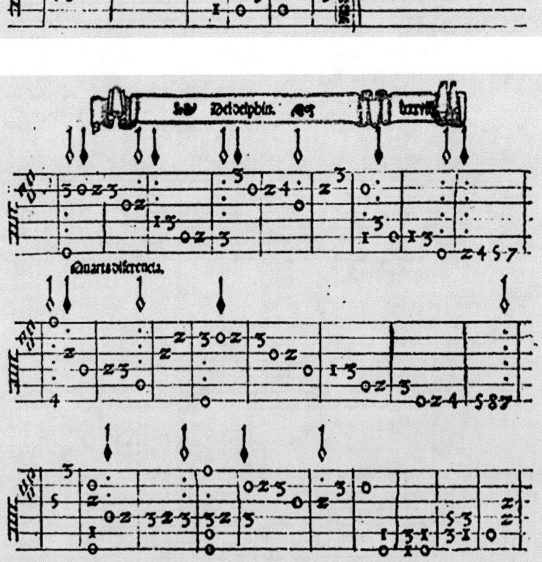

Quarta diferencia.

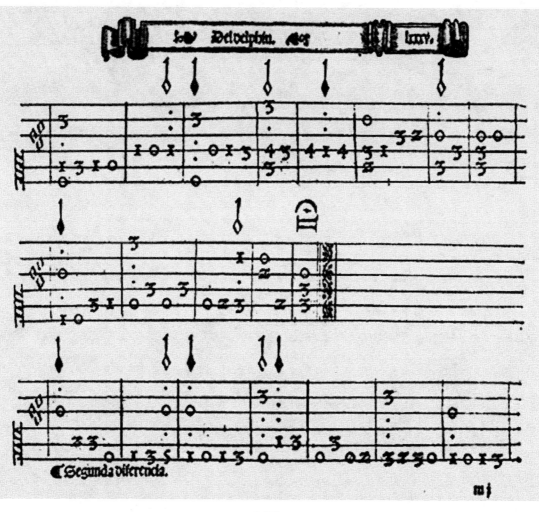

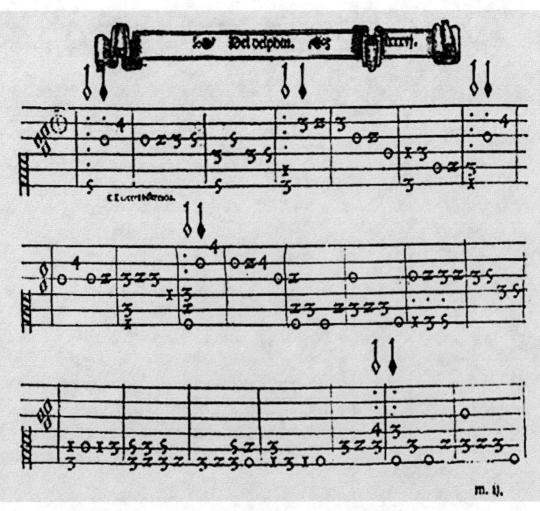

14.4   Alonzo Mudarra: *Pavana, Gallarda*

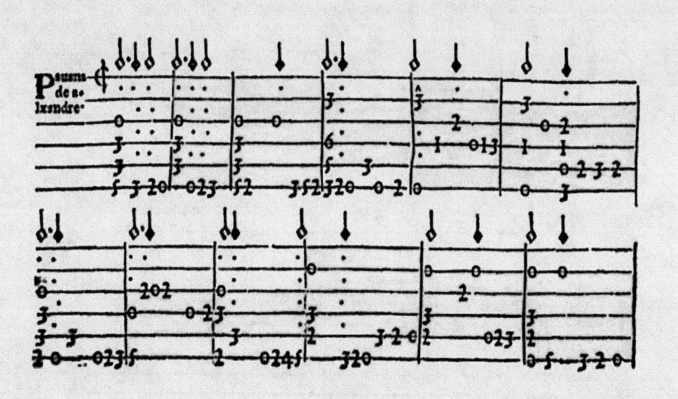

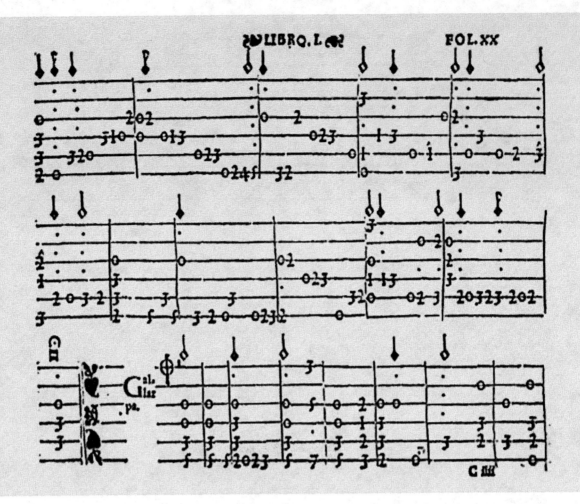

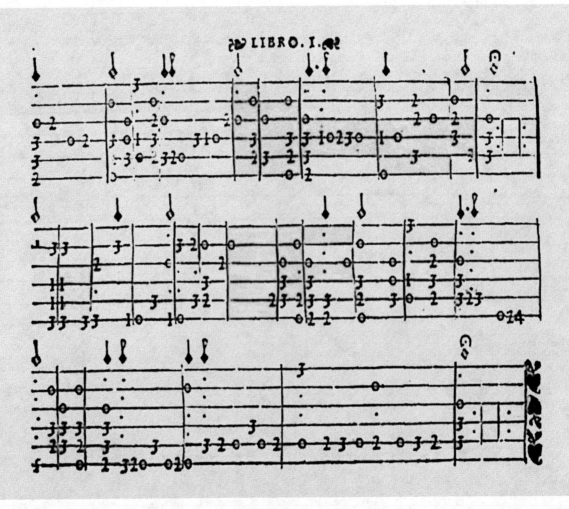

14.5   Alonso Mudarra: *Fantasía 10*

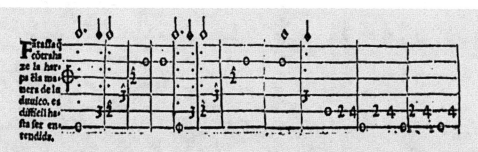

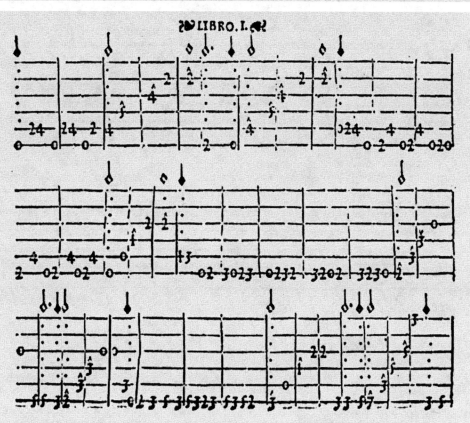

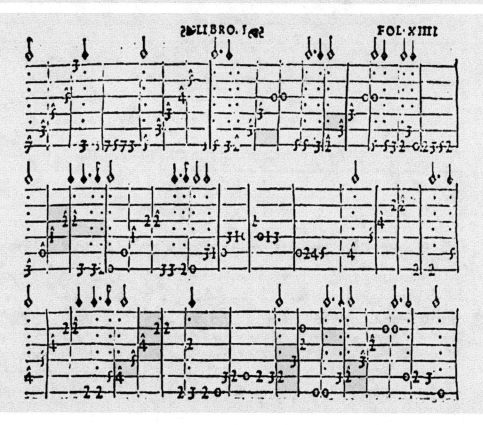

℃ Des de aqui fasta acerca del final ay

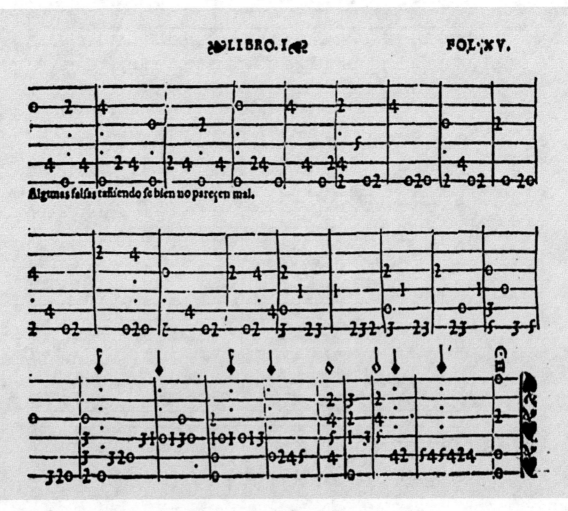

Algunas falsas tañiendo se bien no parecen mal.

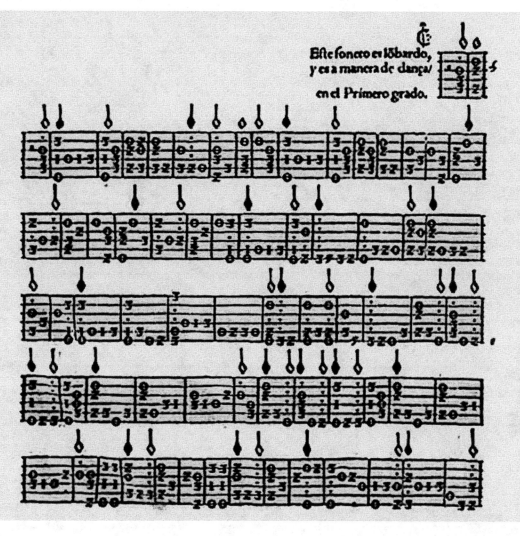

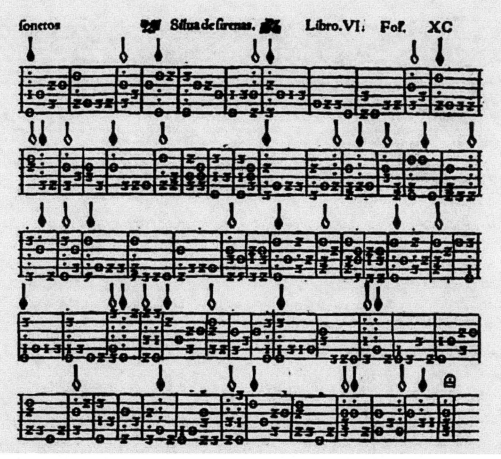

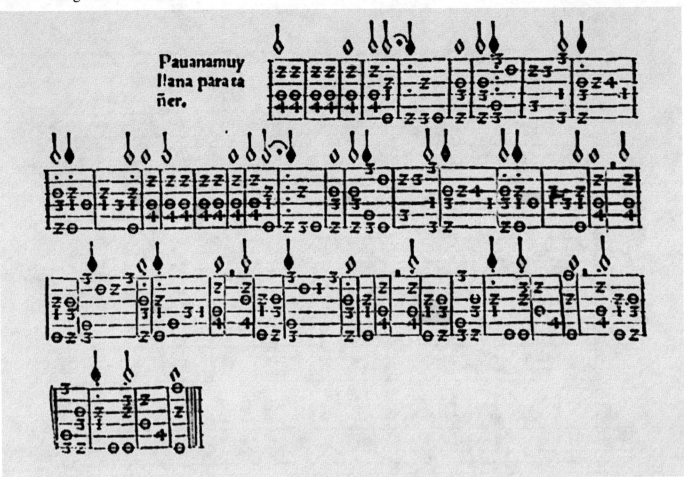

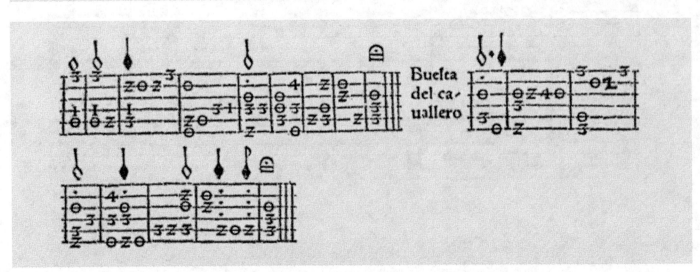

Villancicos.   Libro segundo.   Pisador   Fo. ix.

COMIENCA EL SEGVN
DO LIBRO QVE TRATA DE VILLANCICOS A TRES

para cantar el que quisiere, y sino tañerlos, y son para principiantes. Y otros
a quatro bozes, tambien para tañer. Y otros que se cantan las tres bo
zes, y se canta el tiple que va apuntado encima.

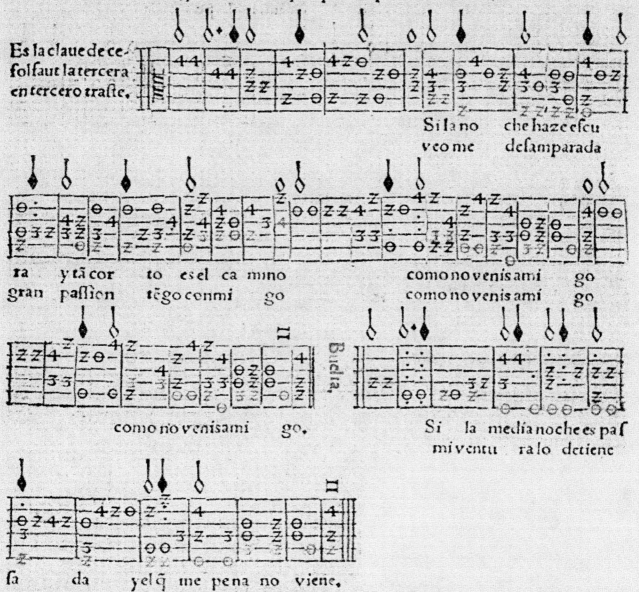

Es la claue de ce
folfaut la tercera
en tercero traste.

Si la no   che haze escu
veo me   desamparada

ra   y tã cor   to es el ca mino   como no venis ami   go
gran   passion   tẽgo con mi   go   como no venis ami   go

como no venis ami   go.

Buelta.

Si   la media noche es pas
mi ventu   ra lo detiene

fa   da   yel q̃ me pena no viene.
per   q̃   foy muy desdi   chada.

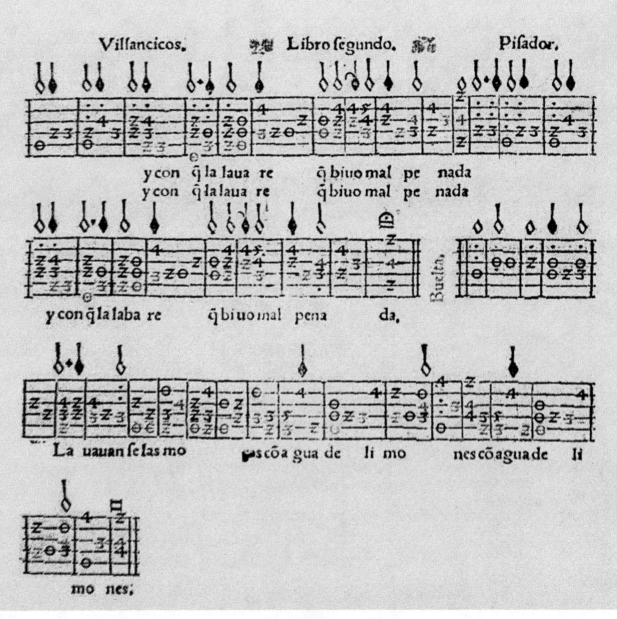

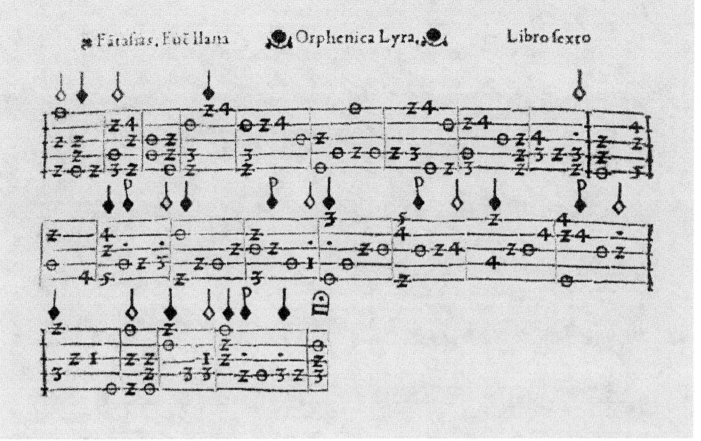

. Libro primero: **Fantaſias**

Fantaſia a 3. por el octauo tono,
ſeñalaſe la claue de Fefaut en la
quarta en vacio.

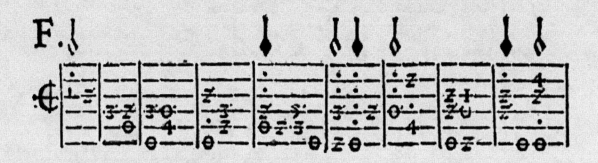

A tres. **Libro primero.** **Fol. 17.**

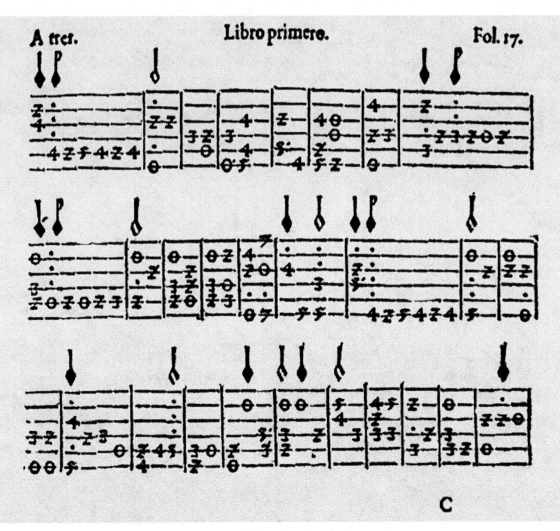

C

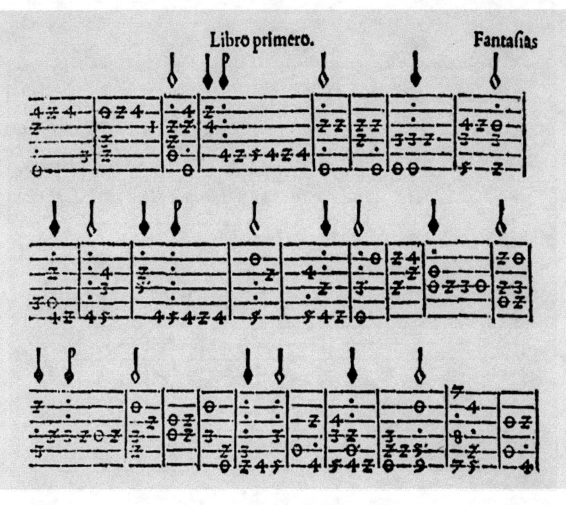

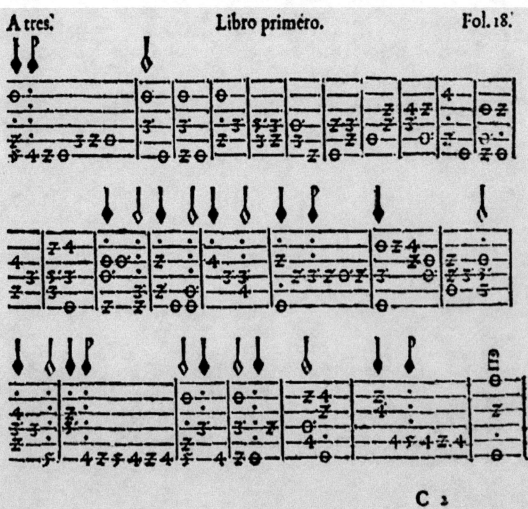

C 2

15. Selected Bibliography

Amos, Nelson. "Luis Narváez, *Guárdame las vacas,* and the *'otra parte'*." *Soundboard,* (Summer 2000): 21-25.

Annoni, Maria Therese. "Tuning, Temperament and Pedagogy for the Vihuela in Juan   Bermudo's *Declaracion de Instrumentos Musicales* (1555)." Ph.D. diss., Ohio State University, 1989.

Binkley, Thomas and Margit Frenk. *Spanish Romances of the Sixteenth Century.* Bloomington: Indiana University Press, 1995.

Bermudo, Juan. *El libro llamado declaracion de instrumentos musicales* (Osuna, 1555). Facsimile reprint. Kassel: Bärenreiter, 1957.

_____. *Juan Bermudo: "On Playing the Vihuela" ("De tañer vihuela") from* Declaracion de instrumentos musicales *(Osuna, 1555).* Dawn Astrid Espinosa, trans. *Journal of the Lute Society of America* 28-29 (1995-1996).

Bermúdez, Egberto. "La vihuela de la Iglesia de la Compañía de Jesús de Quito." *Revista de Musicología* 15 (1992): 97-105.

_____. "La vihuela: Los ejemplares de Paris y Quito." *La guitarra española-The Spanish guitar.* Madrid: Sociedad Estatal Quinto Centenario, 1991, 25-47.

Brown, Howard Mayer. *Instrumental Music Printed before 1608: A Bibliography.* Cambridge, MA: Harvard University Press, 1967.

Chase, Gilbert. *The Music of Spain.* New York: W. W. Norton, 1941. Second edition, revised, New York: Dover Publications, 1959.

Corona-Alcade, Antonio. "A Vihuela Manuscript in the Archivo de Simancas." *The Lute* 26 (1986): 3-20.

_____. "The Earliest Vihuela Tablature: A Recent Discovery." *Early Music* 20 (1992): 594–600.

_____. "The Vihuela and the Guitar in Sixteenth-Century Spain: A critical appraisal of some of the existing evidence." *The Lute* 30 (1990): 3-24.

Creston, Paul. *Rational Metric Notation: The Mathematical Basis of Meters, Symbols, and Note-Values.* Hicksville, NY: Exposition Press, 1979.

Dugot, Joël. "Un nouvel exemplaire de vihuela au Musée de la Musique?" *Luths et luthistes en Occident: Actes du Colloque 13-15 mai 1998.* Paris: Cité de la Musique (1999): 307-317.

Frenk, Margit. *Corpus de la Antigua Lírica Popular Hispánica*. Madrid: Castalia, 1987.

Gásser, Luis. *Luis Milán on Sixteenth-Century Performance Practice*. Bloomington and Indianapolis: Indiana University Press, 1996.

Griffiths, John. "At Court and at Home with the vihuela de mano." *Journal of the Lute Society of America* 22 (1989): 1-27.

_____. "Esteban Daza: A Gentleman Musician in Renaissance Spain." *Early Music* 23, no. 3, (1995): 437-448.

_____. *Esteban Daza: The Fantasias for Vihuela*. Madison: A-R Editions, *Recent Researches in Music of the Renaissance* 54, 1982.

_____. "Extremities: the vihuela in development and decline." *Luths et luthistes en Occident: Actes de colloque 13-15 Mai 1998*. Paris: Cité de la Musique (1999): 51-61.

_____· "Mudarra's Harp Fantasia: History and Analysis," *Australian Guitar Journal* 1 (1989): 19-25.

_____. *Tañer Vihuela Según Juan Bermudo: Polifonía Vocal Y Tablaturas Instrumentales*. Zargoza: Institución "Fernando El Católico," 2003.

_____. "The Two Renaissances of the Vihuela." *Goldberg Magazine*. *www.goldbergweb.com/en/magazine/essays/2005/04/31026.php*.

_____. "The Vihuela Fantasia: A Comparative Study of Forms and Styles." Ph.D. diss., Monash University, Australia, 1984.

_____. "The vihuela: performance practice, style, and context." *Performance on Lute, Guitar, and Vihuela: Historical Practice and Modern Interpretation*. Cambridge: Cambridge University Press, 1997, 173-174.

Escartí, Vicent-Josep and Antonio Tordera. *Lluís del Milà: El Cortesano*. 2 vols. Valencia: Universitat de Valencia, 2001.

Esses, Maurice. *Dance and instrumental Diferencias in Spain During the 17th and 18th Centuries*, 2 vols. Stuyvesant, NY: Pendragon Press, 1992.

Grimes, David. *The Complete Fantasias of Luys Milán*. Pacific, MO: Mel Bay, 2000.

Harder, Thomas Lee. "The Vihuela Fantasias from Miguel de Fuenllana's 'Orphenica Lyra': Introduction and Guitar Transcription of Nine Representative Works." DMA diss., Arizona State University, 1992.

Hearn, Bill. "Playing Devil's Advocate: The Shaky Case for Unison-Course Vihuela Stringing." *Lute Society of America Quarterly*, May/August (1993): 4-10.

Jacobs, Charles. *A Spanish Renaissance Songbook*. University Park: Pennsylvania State University Press, 1988.

_____. *Tempo Notation in Renaissance Spain*. Brooklyn: Institute of Mediaeval Music, 1964.

Koonce, Frank. *The Baroque Guitar in Spain and the New World*. Pacific, MO: Mel Bay Publications, 2006.

_____. "Rhythm vs. Meter." *Soundboard* 32, Nos. 3-4 (2007): 36-43.

Minamino, Hiroyuki. "The viola da mano in Renaissance Italy: A synopsis." *Lute Society of America Quarterly* 34/1 (February 1999): 6-9.

Navarrete, Ignacio. "The Problem of the *Soneto* in the Spanish Renaissance Vihuela Books." *Sixteenth Century Journal* 23, No. 4 (1992): 769-789.

Poulton, Diana. "The Lute in Christian Spain." *The Lute Society Journal* 19 (1977): 34-49.

Russell, Craig H. "The Eight Modes as Tonal Forces in the Music of Luis Milán." *De Música Hispana et Aliis* I (1990): 323-326.

Salinas, Francisco de. *De música Libri septem* (1577). Modern Spanish ed., *Siete libros sobre la música / Francisco Salinas; primera versión castellana por Ismael Fernández de la Cuesta*. Madrid: Alpuerto, 1983.

Sohns, Eduardo. "Seis versions del villancico *Con qué la lavaré* en los cancioneros españoles del siglo XVI." *Revista de Musicología* 10, no. 1, (1987): 173-220.

Smith, Douglas Alton. *A History of the Lute from Antiquity to the Renaissance*. The Lute Society of America, 2002. 221-223.

Ward, John Milton. "The *Vihuela de mano* and its Music, 1536–1576." Ph.D. diss., New York University, 1953.

_____· "Changing the Instrument for the Music." *Journal of the Lute Society of America* 15 (1982): 27-39.

_____· "The Use of Borrowed Material in l6th-Century Instrumental Music," *Journal of the American Musicological Society* 5 (1952): 88-98.

Waters, Eric. *Guitar Music from "Tres Libros de Música."* Pacific, MO: Mel Bay Publications, 2004.

Woodfield, Ian. *The Early History of the Viol*. Cambridge: Cambridge University Press, 1984.

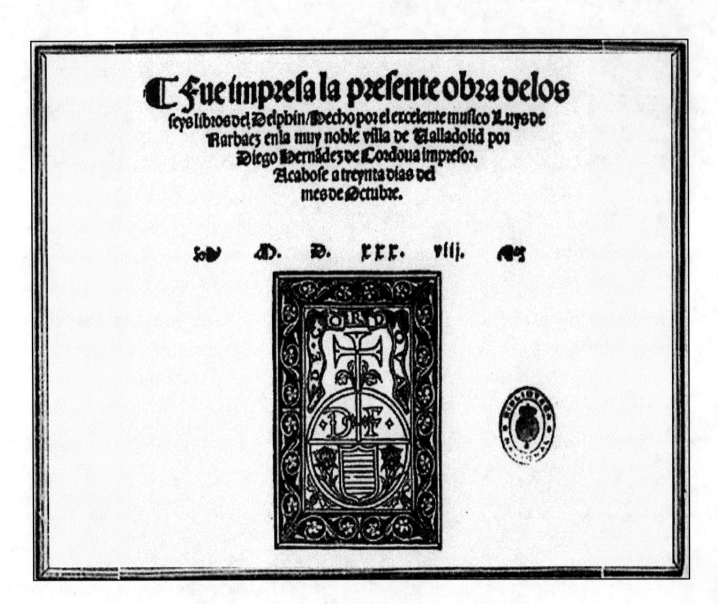

The colophon at the end of Narváez's book that shows the printer's trademark and time and place of publication. The text translates: "The present work of los seys libros del Delphín, made by the excellent musician Luys de Narvaez in the very noble town of Valladolid, was printed by Diego Hernandez de Cordoba, printer. It was finished on the thirtieth day of the month of October, MDXXXVIII (1538)."